FIRST GRADE ▼
B▲SICS

FIRST GRADE ▼ BASICS

KATE KELLY AND ANNE ZEMAN

ILLUSTRATION BY PETER SPACEK

BOOK DESIGN BY ALLEYCAT DESIGN, INC.

THE TASHUA-PRINCETON STUDY GROUP

Jacqueline Norcel

Brian Lally

Allida Finnegan

Jean Marie Mysogland

Janice Coulson

Terry Buckingham

Judy Gallo

Lorraine Dattner

Kate Kelly

Anne Zeman

BLACK DOG & LEVENTHAL PUBLISHERS • NEW YORK

Published by

Black Dog & Leventhal Publishers, Inc.
151 West 19th Street
New York, New York 10011

Distributed by

Workman Publishing Company
708 Broadway
New York, New York 10003

Manufactured in the United States of America

ISBN: 1-884822-12-6

For Kendra, who inspired and mastered the basics.

ACKNOWLEDGMENTS

Many thanks to the teachers, counselors, parents and children who read, responded to, and tested the activities in this and the other *Basics* books, especially: Kendra, Erin, Megan, Maura, Bill, Alanna, Keara, Brooke, Amber, and the student body of Tashua School.

Thanks, too, to Mary Jo Battistelli and Sovanni Bun for getting the manuscripts together, to Pam Horn, a patient editor with a kind blue pencil, and to J.P. Leventhal for believing in *Basics*.

CONTENTS

FOREWORD

As a teacher for thirty-five years, I realize that vision, commitment, and education count most at the family and community levels. Only through the enduring partnership of families, educators, and other dedicated citizens can America's learning enterprise—our local schools—unleash our children's full potential.

Until the completion of high school, a child spends only thirteen percent of his or her waking hours in school—so it is logical that activities outside of school have a dramatic impact on learning. Numerous studies focusing on the home-school connection have shown that parents' active support of a child's education can add as much as half a year's progress to every school year.

The *Basics* series is designed to help parents support the educational process through projects and activities that sharpen skills, focus goals, and provide a sense of accomplishment. And learning has never been so much fun. With *Basics*, you enter into the process right along with your kids, demonstrating the pleasure and importance of reading, writing, and mathematics in everyday life. And when you instill a love of learning, you lay the groundwork for your child's entire future.

Remember, children develop and learn in many different ways, and at different rates. All children have ups and downs in learning. Your support and encouragement—and your participation—are key to insuring your child's continuing development.

Parents can be extraordinary teachers. I invite you to use *Basics* to help your child identify strengths, set realistic goals, and discover his or her true potential.

Jacqueline J. Norcel
Principal, Tashua School

Jacqueline J. Norcel, Chair of the Tashua-Princeton Study Group and Principal of Tashua School in Trumbull, Connecticut, holds B.S. and M.S. degrees in education, as well as an Ed.D. degree. She is the recipient of numerous professional awards and service commendations, including the National Distinguished Principals Award. Under her stewardship, Tashua School was named a National Exemplary School by the United States Department of Education.

Since 1985, Ms. Norcel has served as Adjunct Professor in the Department of Education at Sacred Heart University in Connecticut, and has written articles, speeches, and lectures on primary education and parent-teacher collaboration in education.

FIRST GRADE BASICS

INTRODUCTION

W hy can't Jenny read? Why are our children outpaced in math and sciences by the youth of other developed and emerging nations? What has brought about the decline of education in our country?

Over the past several years, these questions have fueled considerable debate among educators, psychologists, anthropologists, social historians, politicians, and parents. Johnny can't read because classroom standards have slipped away in our public schools. But how can our teachers compete when budget cuts leave them with unwieldy class sizes and spare, inferior, or obsolete materials?

Among the consequences of our national concern about the state of education is a proliferation of books and articles pinpointing various reasons for and solutions to the problem. Popular among the reasons proferred is that, because our children suffer from a lack of common background coming into school and this lack continues because of differences in state-to-state curricula, our children can't be educated efficiently. The suggested solution lies in providing our children with more culturally and educationally uniform backgrounds from preschool through the primary grades. This philosophy has spawned a popular series of books for parents and teachers, a series that attempts to outline what the elements of a uniform educational program are.

But many parents and teachers reject the notion of educational uniformity, emphasizing instead the need for diversity and multiculturalism in education. Proponents of multicultural approaches often argue that, in order to break down the barriers of prejudice and misunderstanding, diversity must be taught, that acceptance comes through knowledge and awareness.

In the meantime, who's supposed to be teaching? If our children aren't learning in school, should our children be schooled in the home? Is it incumbent on parents with school-age children—even those in the best of school systems and with the most promising academic futures—to evaluate their children's academic progress and tutor them in their curricular subjects?

The *Basics* series doesn't attempt to answer these questions, nor does it represent an approach to solving the problems in American education. Instead, *Basics* is geared to reinforce fundamental learning skills—skills above debate and widely embraced as essential to success in school. The series is written on the premise that parents should not have to be teachers, but that parents can and should introduce and reinforce learning by encouraging their children to play skill-related games and activities.

Rather than extend the classroom into the kitchen, keep the the kitchen for family fun. Games and activities exercise the critical-thinking, problem-solving, and other curriculum-related skills essential to your child's success in school. You don't need a teaching certificate or a degree in education to help your child learn. You simply need interest in your child's education and the time and simple materials to encourage productive play.

WHY BASICS?

Basics in the series title refers to basic learning skills, skills that despite the debate and controversy in education are recognized as fundamental, and skills that are encouraged and developed in the school program. Ideally, home learning is consistent with the school program. But at home as well as at school, effective learning combines several characteristics:

- Learning is an active, not a passive process. Children learn better from doing and telling than by being told.

- Learning comes naturally from experience. Real-life experiences are the best basis for learning.

- Learning has a holistic nature. The process is based on mastering foundational systems rather than focusing on specific, small tasks.

- Learning comes from activities and games that meet a child's needs and interests.

- Learning involves making choices.

- Learning motivates interaction with people and materials, develops self-reliance and attention span.

BASICS AND GRADE LEVELS

To foster age-appropriate skill development, the *Basics* series is divided into volumes based on grade levels. This method provides an easy reference point and, for the most part, will guide you to the appropriate volume for you and your child. Within each volume, skills sets are the topics of individual chapters. Within these chapters, activities become progressively more complicated. The objective is to introduce a skill, reinforce it, and then make using it challenging and fun. Although a child may be unable to do activities at the beginning of a school year, he or she will be better able by year's end. Some activities almost certainly require parental guidance and supervision. These activities are accompanied by a parent icon.

Although the *Basics* volumes outline a variety of activities for different interests and abilities, be sure the *Basics* volume you choose is appropriate. This is especially important in the early primary grades, where physical and mental development can vary widely from one child to the next. Your child may not be ready for the activities in his or her "grade level" *Basics* book, or may be ready for the next "grade level."

BASICS, YOU, AND YOUR CHILD

The texts in all the *Basics* volumes address the child, not the parent. The introductions and chapter overviews, however, describe the learning skills emphasized and the particular purpose of each activity for the parent. Consequently, *Basics* books are written for both children and parents. While providing a guidebook for fun, they also provide a thumbnail of grade-specific learning objectives.

DOWN TO BASICS

The activities and games in *Basics* require only simple materials—pencils, paper, cardboard, markers, paints, and recycled household materials. The purpose of limiting supplies is to make the activities easy and accessible to as wide an audience as possible. For those fortunate enough to have them, other materials-building systems, such as Lego® or Tinker Toys®, Colorforms®, two- and three-dimensional puzzles, modelling clays, etc.—are wonderful for creative learning. So, too, are cameras, calculators, and computers and the myriad educational software programs on disks and CD-ROM. Many of the *Basics* activities can be adapted to these materials, and much of the computer learning software available concentrates on developing many of the same skills.

In addition to the activities, each *Basics* book includes a section listing "Good Books to Read." These lists were compiled by the Tashua-Princeton Study Group. The criteria for selection included awards (Caldecott, Newbury, etc.), popularity among school children, availability (in print), and frequency of appearance on selected school and public library recommended reading lists. It is by no means comprehensive, but introduces a variety of authors and titles appropriate to early primary readers and listeners. Reading is essential to success in every school subject. Foster a love of reading in your child by reading to him or her as often as possible. Continue family reading throughout the school grades.

1

LANGUAGE LOVERS ONLY, PLEASE!

READING AND LITERATURE

OVERVIEW FOR PARENTS

At the beginning of the school year, your first-grader may be able to read a few words, or maybe even a story or book. By year's end, he or she will have mastered several stories and beginner texts.

Reading requires several skills—sorting, ordering, differentiation, sequencing, phonics, memory, and more. Many of these skills were introduced, reinforced, and mastered in kindergarten. But another skill—listening—is also fundamental to reading. That's why primary schoolteachers read to their classes—

and why parents should read to their children, even if the children can read by themselves. When you read to your child, discuss the pictures, predict what will happen next, and ask questions to make sure he or she is an active listener.

Now that your child is reading, you should listen, too. You can come to understand a great deal about your child's learning style by observing his or her reading. Does your child read with a logical flow, modulating the voice and pausing appropriately? How does your child handle new or difficult words? Does your child remember the main ideas of what's read? The details?

In this chapter are several activities geared to help your child practice and master basic reading skills, from rhyming to deductive reasoning. In between, sound and word recognition, problem solving, and critical thinking are part of the fun.

1. RHYME TIME

These activities borrow familiar rhymes to help your child recognize and read words. "Blank Verse" let's your child read picture clues to fill in the blanks in some favorite poetry. If your child doesn't know the verses, use the same technique, writing out poems but leaving blanks for your child to fill in. Then ask your child to match the missing word to a spelled-out list.

"Rhyming Pairs" is an aural skills game. Although rhyming is practiced in kindergarten, many children, while familiar with rhyme, haven't mastered it by first grade. It's an important phonics skill, one that helps not only with reading, but also with spelling and composition.

"Rhyming Lists" organizes "Rhyming Pairs" into word "families." For example, the *at* family includes cat, fat, mat, etc. This activity may be too difficult during the first few months of first grade. If you want to practice the skill but also want to save your child some frustration, create "family" cards: *at, in, all, am, en, et, it, og, up, etc.* Then, use alphabet cards to form words with the family cards. You might put a *P* alphabet card next to the *at* family card to form *pat,* then move the *P* next to the *en* family card to form *pen,* or next to *it* to form *pit,* etc. Then change the alphabet card from *P* to *B* to form *bat,* to *C* to form *cat,* etc.

"Search and Destroy" is too difficult for many first-graders until later in the year. It's a game that is appropriate for second- and even third-graders, too. As your child becomes more familiar with poetry forms and rhyming, he or she will be able to construct more complicated rhyming pairs.

2. LABEL THE FABLE

These activities assume a knowledge of Aesop's fables. If your child has heard these stories, he or she will find it easier to match each fable to the lesson it teaches than the child who is hearing these tales for the first time. Regardless of your child's familiarity with the fables, guide him or her through the stories and offer examples from modern life to illustrate their lessons.

You might also ask your child if he or she can think of a story to fit Aesop's morals.

The lessons in fables and adages may seem clear to us, but they can confound a first-grader. While activities in the section provide a valuable exercise in deductive reasoning and critical thinking, don't overdo. Start slowly, one fable or adage at a time. That's more than enough for a young mind to absorb.

3. PICTURE THIS

"Picture This" helps your child sort information and reconstruct stories. It also helps him or her to visualize the main events or episodes in favorite stories. As with the nursery rhymes and fables in the first activity sets in this chapter, familiarity with the stories is helpful to your child's success. If your child is unfamiliar with the fairy tales used here, either use another story or first read the stories in more complete versions. These are easily found in many collections of children's stories. Once your child knows the plots and characters well, ask him or her to match the titles, retell the tales, and create a personal fairy tale album.

"Serial Storytelling," unlike "Story Hour" and "Personal Fairy Tales," does not rely on old favorites. Encourage your child to make up original tales assuming, of course, that elements from other fairy tales will be borrowed.

If you encourage "High Drama," be prepared to help! Organizing a play is a big challenge for your young first-grader. But it's very rewarding, too, and well worth your guidance and assistance.

4. WHO DONE IT?

Stories are written to tell about a problem and the solution to that problem. Good stories have problems and solutions that are believable and interesting. Here we focus on mysteries, stories that hinge entirely on problems and problem-solving.

In these activities, your child's logic skills get a workout. First, a problem is presented. But what caused the problem? See if your child can work out some plausible reasons. Then, see if he or she is up to concocting solutions.

"Who Done It?" should be challenging for most first-graders. Be sure to offer advice when it's needed.

5. SCAT(TERED) CAT(EGORIES)

The activities in "Scat(tered) Cat(egories)" are designed to reinforce sorting and association skills while developing vocabulary and fine motor skills. "Toss Up Topics" requires quick response to sorting and association challenges. If the game is too difficult for your first-grader, make this association activity simpler by eliminating the clap-and-snap sequence. Once your child has a better grasp of sorting and associations, introduce the clapping.

"Face It Face Down" combines sorting with memory and concentration skills. This game is very tricky. You child isn't likely to become frustrated, however, because incorrect results produce amusing pictures anyway. This activity is a word-free activity geared for pre- and post-reading first-graders. It's also a warm-up for "Scattered Cats." "Scattered Cats" uses the concentration skills in "Face It Face Down" and applies them to words and ideas. You can modify this activity for the pre-reader by using picture cards instead of word cards.

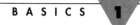

RHYME TIME

"BLANK" VERSE

See if you can figure out these favorite poems by using the picture clues.

PICTURE CLUES:

Old Mother Hubbard

Went to the

To get her poor   a

But when she got there,

The   was bare,

And so her poor   had none.

PICTURE AND WORD CLUES

cupboard

dog

bone

PICTURE CLUES:

Twinkle, twinkle, little ,

How I wonder what you are.

Up above the so high

Like a in the .

Twinkle, twinkle, little ,

How I wonder what you are.

star

world

diamond

sky

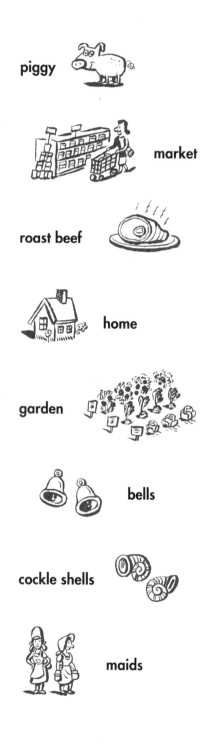

piggy

market

roast beef

home

garden

bells

cockle shells

maids

PICTURE CLUES:

This little 🐷 went to 🏪 ,

This little 🐷 stayed 🏠 ,

This little 🐷 ate 🍖 ,

This little 🐷 had none,

And this little 🐷 cried wee-wee-wee

All the way 🏠 .

PICTURE CLUES:

Mary, Mary, quite contrary,

How does your 🌷 grow?

With silver 🔔 , and 🐚 ,

And pretty 👧👧 all in a row.

RHYMING PAIRS

Stuck in the car with nothing to do? Rainy outside and no place to go? Waiting at the restaurant for your spaghetti to come? Why not pass the time with a few rounds of "Rhyming Pairs." All you need is a pal or two to play with you.

First, say a word, any word.

Next, have the second player say a word that rhymes with your word—and makes a rhyming pair. For example, you might say "stair," and the next player might say "underwear!" That's a rhyming pair:

stair
underwear

If only two of you are playing, simply take turns stating words to rhyme. If you're playing with three or more, a player who cannot form a rhyming pair is out of the game. The last player remaining in the game wins.

RHYMING LISTS

Once you've played a few rounds of "Rhyming Pairs," you'll be ready to build some "Rhyming Lists."

You'll need:
a pencil • paper

EDWARD LEAR

Some writers are best known for nonsense. One of the best-known nonsense writers is Edward Lear.

Lear was born in London, England, in 1812. He was the 20th child in a wealthy family. But young Lear's early fortune turned bad. At age seven, he began to suffer from epilepsy and six years later, his father fell into debt. Lear and his brothers and sisters had to go to work.

By the time he was 19, Lear was at work as an illustrator, drawing the parrots at the London Zoo. His work was in such favor that the Earl of Derby hired him to draw all of his animals. While he was staying at the earl's estate, Lear illustrated some limericks he made up for the earl's grandchildren. These were published in 1846 under the title *The Book of Nonsense.*

First, think of a word you know. You might think cat. Then think of all the words you know that rhyme with cat and write them down on a piece of paper. Ask for help if you don't know how to write all the words.

Then, move on to another word. Take a new sheet of paper to record the word and its rhymes.

Don't worry if you can't think of more than two or three rhymes for a word. Some lists will be longer than others.

Save your rhyming lists in an old shoebox or notebook. You can make rhyming lists any time you feel like it and add the lists to your box or book. Once you have a collection of rhyming lists, you can play "Search and Destroy"—a rhyming game guaranteed to change your favorite rhymes and poems.

For a little variation, record your rhyming lists on a cassette tape. You can play back your rhymes and listen closely to how they sound.

SEARCH AND DESTROY

Search for the rhymes in your favorite poems. Then replace them with your own rhymes. Chances are you'll destroy the old standards—but create new masterpieces of your own.

> **You'll need:**
> **rhyming lists**

First, choose a poem or piece of verse with rhyming lines.

Old Mother Hubbard
Went to the cupboard
To get her poor dog a bone,
But when she got there,
The cupboard was bare,
And so her poor dog had none.

Lear's book was a great success. Once again enjoying good fortune, he spent his adult life traveling, writing, and illustrating such nonsense as:

There was an Old Man with a nose,
Who said, "If you choose to suppose
"That my nose is too long,
"You are certainly wrong!"
That remarkable man with a nose.

Then, using your "Rhyming Lists," replace the rhyming words in the poem with words from your lists. At first, you might want to make up nonsense poems. After a while, try to make your re-rhymed versions make sense. You may have to change a line or two, as well as the rhyming words.

Last, recite your masterpieces of rhyme for family and friends.

RHYMING LISTS:

boom	soon
broom	spoon
room	tune
zoom	

Old Mother ~~Hubbard~~ Zoom
Went to her ~~cupboard~~ room
To get her poor ~~dog~~ cat a ~~bone~~ spoon.
When she got ~~there~~ one
The ~~cupboard cat was bare~~ had some fun
~~And so the poor dog had none~~ Clicking a rhythmical tune.

RHYMING LISTS:

bell	cell
dell	fell
gel	shell
smell	spell
well	

~~Twinkle, twinkle,~~ Stinky, stinky little ~~star~~ Well,
How I wonder ~~where you are.~~ what's that smell.
~~Up above the sky so high~~
In deep water standing still
~~Like a diamond in the sky.~~
Is odor that will make me ill.
~~Twinkle, twinkle,~~ Stinky, stinky little ~~star~~ Well,
How I wonder ~~where you are.~~ what's that smell.

LABEL THE FABLE

Do you know what a fable is? It's a special kind of story, usually an animal story, that teaches a lesson, or *moral*. If you've heard the fables below, you'll be able to match them up with the lessons they teach.

THE BOY WHO CRIED WOLF

A shepherd boy watched a flock of sheep for the villagers. He needed to protect them from the wolves that lived in the forest nearby. The wolves might eat the sheep and then the villagers would be short of food.

Morning soon became afternoon. As the day grew longer, the shepherd boy grew bored. He wondered what would happen if he cried, "Wolf!" And so he did.

The villagers came running to help the boy protect the sheep. Worried and out of breath, they found no wolf, only a bored shepherd boy amazed at their concern. The villagers turned angry and warned the boy never to cry "Wolf!" again.

But the days passed, and the shepherd boy grew tired of his job again. He wondered what might happen if, today, he cried, "Wolf!" And so he did.

Again the villagers came running. And again they returned angry at the boy's silly prank, warning him as they left never, ever to cry out unless there was a real wolf.

Then one day, as the shepherd boy was tending the flocks, a real wolf came. The boy cried out, "Wolf, wolf, wolf!" but the villagers didn't come. The boy cried again, yet no one came. Many of the sheep were eaten and he could do nothing about it. At last the shepherd understood that to cry "Wolf!" was a silly—and dangerous—prank.

—Aesop

THE TORTOISE AND THE HARE

The hare was one of the fastest animals in the forest, and he loved to brag about his speed to the tortoise, a slow-moving but earnest fellow.

One day, the tortoise had had enough teasing. He challenged the hare to a race. "I may be slow," the tortoise said, "but I just might beat you to the main road."

The hare was quick to agree to the race. Within minutes, the hare was way ahead of the tortoise. He was so far ahead, in fact, that he decided to take a little nap. Soon the hare was sound asleep. He heard not a sound as the tortoise passed his sleeping body and moved ahead toward the main road.

The hare awoke with a start. Realizing he'd overslept, he raced as fast as he could toward the finish line—just in time to see the tortoise win the race. The tortoise was pleased to point out, "Slow and steady wins the race!"

—Aesop

THE MAID AND THE MILK PAIL

One day, a maid set off to market with a pail of fresh milk. She was to sell the milk and return home with the empty pail and the milk money in her pocket.

But as she walked along the road, she thought she might buy some fat hens with the milk money. The hens would lay eggs and hatch more chickens. Then she could take the chickens to the market and sell them for an even better price than the milk.

With the extra money from the chickens, the maid thought she might buy a fresh blue ribbon for her hair. Then, she thought, all the boys would think her pretty and want to dance with her at the spring fair.

The maid was so deep in her thoughts that she forgot about her milk pail. Pretending to dance, she twirled round and the milk spilled out on the ground.

The maid returned home with an empty pail and no money to show for it. She told her mother the whole story. Her mother comforted her and advised, "Don't count your chickens before they're hatched."

—Aesop

AESOP

Little is known about the life of Aesop, although most scholars believe he was born about 620 B.C. in Phrygia, a country in ancient Asia. Aesop served as a slave in the home of a Greek man named Iadmon.

MORALS

Match the following traditional morals with their modern version interpretations.

Traditional Morals

1. Don't cry wolf.
2. Slow and steady wins the race.
3. Don't count your chickens before they are hatched.

Modern Morals

A. Don't hope for things to go exactly as you plan because you might be disappointed.

B. If you often are untruthful, people will stop believing you—even if you're telling the truth.

C. Having talent doesn't mean you'll always be a success.

Answers: 1-B 2-C 3-A

FABLE-LOUS WORDS

Have you heard any of these lines and lessons? They're difficult to understand—unless you can think of an example or two to illustrate them.

Practice what you preach.

Don't put off for tomorrow what you can do today.

Look before you leap.

A penny saved is a penny earned.

A stitch in time saves nine.

Aesop watched and listened to the people in Iadmon's house. Then he began to tell stories about Greek life, although he disguised the characters by changing them into talking animals. The stories were so good, Iadmon called upon Aesop to tell them to his guests.

What did the authors of these great lines really mean? Ask someone you think might know to talk about the lines with you.

News of the great storyteller spread to the emperor, who called Aesop to live in his palace. There Aesop lived out his days, telling his fables about animals—and always offering a moral, or lesson, at the end.

GET THE PICTURE?

Not all lessons have to come from famous lines. Think about the lines below. Can you think up a story that fits these lessons? Can you think of your own story with a lesson at the end?

Why not draw a picture to help you tell your fable.

You'll need:
drawing paper • a pencil, crayons, or markers

Don't pet a dog you don't know.

It's better to look at all the options before making a choice.

PICTURE THIS

STORY HOUR

You've probably heard your favorite bedtime story so many times that you could tell it—detail for detail. And should anyone who reads to you leave out a line or two, you certainly can fill in the missing words or ideas.

Take a look at the cartoons of some frequently told fairy tales. Do you recognize the stories from the pictures? Can you match the titles at right with the following picture series?

STORY TITLES:

Rapunzel
Pinocchio
Hansel and Gretel
The Little Mermaid
Rumpelstiltskin

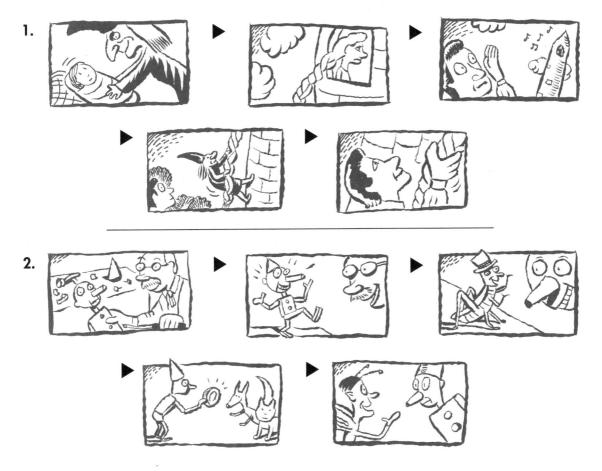

Once you've figured out the stories from the pictures, use the pictures to tell the story to someone else.

PERSONAL FAIRY TALES

Tell your own fairy tale in pictures.

You'll need:
paper • a pencil, crayons, or markers

First, think up a story.

Then, decide how many pictures you want to draw to tell the story.

Next, draw the pictures. Use a separate sheet of paper for each picture.

Last, use your pictures to tell your fairy tale.

Save your pictures! You can put all the fairy tale stories you create in pictures into one big book.

GREAT FIGURES IN FAIRY TALES

The Brothers Grimm and Hans Christian Andersen

Jakob Grimm was born one year before his brother, Wilhelm, in 1785. The sons of a wealthy lawyer, both brothers attended college and studied for civil service jobs. But they found a shared interest in folklore and, instead, made their careers collecting and retelling the stories they heard in songs, poems, and tall tales.

Among the most beloved fairy tales recorded by the Brothers Grimm are *Hansel and Gretel, Snow White, Cinderella,* and *Little Red Riding Hood.* Wilhelm died in 1859, and Jakob in 1863.

Hans Christian Andersen was born in 1805, the son of a poor shoemaker who died when Andersen was only 11 years old. Andersen left school to earn money, only to return to study among 12-year-olds when he was already 17. Andersen was teased for being too tall and gawky to be a schoolboy. Rather than give in to the hurt of his classmates' jeers, he wrote stories about them instead. Andersen, clearly something of a misfit, may have written *The Ugly Duckling* in response to his difficult school years.

SERIAL STORYTELLING

Here's a game that is sure to pass the time while traveling or color the moments of a gray afternoon. All you need is an imagination and a pal or two to keep the story going.

First, decide who'll begin.

Then, have the first storyteller begin a tale, introducing his or her main character and leading up to a dramatic point where the next storyteller takes over.

Continue passing along the storytelling until a storyteller creates a good ending for the tale. It could be minutes, it could be hours. If you've got enough time, start another round of "Serial Storytelling."

HIGH DRAMA

Retell your favorite stories by acting them out with your friends.

You'll need:
a stage area • costumes and props

Andersen published plays and novels, but was best known for his children's stories. Among his other beloved fairy tales are *The Little Mermaid, Thumbelina,* and *The Emperor's New Clothes.* He died in 1875.

First, decide who is playing which character and choose a narrator to introduce the story. Each player should come up with a costume for his or her character, and the props needed to tell the story.

Then, work out what you're going to say. The lines don't have to be the same each time, but they should get across the same idea. The narrator can explain what's happening when the characters aren't talking. Also, work out actions to go with the lines.

Next, practice to be sure you remember what to say and do.

Last, get an audience together. It's showtime!

WHO DONE IT?

Do you like a good mystery? If you do, you'll probably enjoy finding solutions to the problems in the following picture stories. There are no right or wrong answers. Simply use the pictures to find clues to answer the questions.

Mommy is frowning. Baby is crying. Fido is howling. Why are they upset?

The elephants are running away. The cat comes closer.
The hawks circle in the sky, What's going on?

MAKE UP A MYSTERY

Can you tell stories to go with the mystery pictures? Think up
a tale and tell it.

SCAT(TERED) CAT(EGORIES)

Have you ever lost your favorite pajamas or your lucky socks? You looked in the dresser drawer where they're always kept, but they weren't there. Then you dumped out the laundry hamper, but they weren't there. Then you peeked in the washing machine, checked the dryer, and looked through the clean, folded wash. No pajamas. No socks.

A few weeks later, while removing your favorite jeans from their drawer, what do you find? Those missing pajamas, the socks that simply couldn't be found. Oops! They must have been put away in the wrong place.

How well do you organize your clothes? Toys? Storybooks? How well can your organize words and ideas? Try some of the activities that follow and find out.

TOSS UP TOPICS

Try this clapping game with your friends to see how many words you know to fit different topics. First, learn the "Toss Up Topics" jingle:

> **Toss Up Topics,**
> **Arctic to the tropics,**
> **Toss Up Topics now begins**
> **Starting with the topics.**

Then, learn to recite the jingle to a clap-and-snap sequence. Begin by clapping both hands on your knees, then clapping both hands together, and finally snapping twice. Clap and snap in an even rhythm.

Toss [clap knees] **Up** [clap hands] **To-** [snap once]
-pics [snap second time]
Artic [clap knees] **to the** [clap hands] **tro-** [snap once]
-pics [snap second time]
Toss Up [clap knees] **Topics** [clap hands] **now be-** [snap once]
-gins [snap second time]
Starting [clap knees] **with the** [clap hands] **to-** [snap once]
-pics [snap second time]

Next, the players recite the snap-and-clap jingle together and continue snapping and clapping. During the first snap-and-clap sequence following the jingle, one player declares a topic, for example, cars. Play continues to the right. After the topic is declared, the next player has one snap-and-clap sequence to name something related to the topic, for example, wheels. If a player is unable to name something that fits the topic within the snap-and-clap sequence, that player is out of the round. The jingle is recited again by the remaining players, and a new topic is declared. The last player remaining in the game wins.

FACE IT FACE DOWN

Can you put together a picture puzzle—without looking at the picture pieces? See if you can "Face It Face Down."

You'll need:
9 index cards • a marker

First, lay out the index cards into a square. Be sure the edges are touching.

Then, using the marker, draw a face on the index cards. Be sure to mark each card with some part of the picture.

Next, gather the index cards into a deck and shuffle. Then, without looking, lay out the cards face down into a square.

Last, flip each card one by one and place it face down where you think it belongs. Once you've replaced all the cards, flip them over and see if you reconstructed your picture.

For a variation, draw a picture of a pet, house, landscape, bike—anything you want—on the index cards. Then see if you can "Face It Face Down" using your special pictures.

SCATTERED CATS

How good are you at sorting? Can you sort without peeking?

You'll need:
index cards • a marker

First, select three topics. For example, you might choose pets, toys, and school things.

Then, using a marker, write down one word on each index card that relates to your topics. For example, for pets, you might write: dogs, cats, birds, rabbits, gerbils, and frogs; for toys: tops, dolls, sand shovel, swing set. For school things: books, pencils, erasers, desks, backpacks.

Next, collect the index cards into a deck and shuffle. Place the shuffled deck face down.

Then, draw the cards one at a time and sort them face down into topic piles.

Last, check the sorted piles to see how well you unscattered the "Scattered Cats." To make "Scattered Cats" more difficult, increase the number of topics.

THE WRITE STUFF

LANGUAGE AND WRITING SKILLS

During the first grade year, your child will be encouraged not only to read, but also to write. For success in first grade, your child should begin the school year with aural mastery of about 50 words:

top, next to, through, first, front, away from, most, some, part, widest, corner, behind, now, between, bottom, every, end, over, starting, side, last, whole, different, after, beginning, as many, several, other, farthest, second, alike, never, match, always, before, forward, center, medium-sized, right, half, separated, skip, left, third, narrowest, fewest, and pair

By the end of the year, your child should be familiar enough with these words to read most and write many of them.

Compared with the writing and concepts your child can hear, read, and comprehend, your child's writing will seem simple and disorganized. By the end of the first grade year, however, most students have been taught how to form sentences—beginning with a capital letter and ending with a period. The children may also be familiar with using commas to separate items in a list. Most are also introduced to basic parts of speech: nouns, verbs, and adjectives.

Practice and guidance will help your child develop better writing skills. Also, in most cases, the more a child reads and is read to, the better the child will write.

In this chapter, activities are designed to help you encourage your child to write words—words he or she knows, sees, is curious about, or makes up. Writing should be fun. These activities encourage your child to communicate with pencil on paper as well as verbally.

1. THE NAME GAME

One of the easiest ways for your child to write words is to copy them from familiar books, magazines, toy boxes, games, cans, or cartons. Encourage your child to trace or copy words. Ask to see copied words and explain what the words are, and, if necessary, what they mean. With repetition, your first-grader will begin to recognize and write many familiar names and words.

Once your child has mastered "Copy Shop," try "Four-Word Fantasy." For variety and a little color, have your child clip pictures from magazines and newspapers to illustrate the "Four-Word Fantasy." The clipped art can also be used to practice story-telling. The images may inspire your child to write a caption, sentence, paragraph—or even a whole story! Encourage your child to write as much as he or she is capable of without straining. At the beginning of the first grade year, a caption is challenge enough. By the end of the year, your child may well be able to write a few paragraphs.

"Alpha Draw" and "Alpha Snake" review alphabetical order—essential for developing dictionary skills. Ultimately, your first grade writer will find a need for a good beginner's dictionary, and will need to know a-b-c sequence in order to use it!

"Sore Throat" is quite advanced for many first-graders—probably too difficult for the early months of the school year. It's a good game to introduce when you feel your child is ready—and keep playing it through second and even third grade. "Sore Throat" is always a challenge, and it encourages your child to communicate through writing—instead of animated speech—a whole variety of thoughts, feelings, and needs.

2. PEOPLE, PLACES, THINGS, AND ACTIONS

Fundamental to writing is knowing how different words work together to communicate observations, thoughts, ideas, and feelings. While your first-grader learns to read words, he or she also learns to sort words and combine them in sequence to form sentences.

In this set of activities, three parts of speech are introduced: nouns, verbs, and adjectives. With these three types of words, your first-grader can create hundreds or thousands of sentences.

Leave teaching the rules of grammar to the teacher, but, when you feel your first-grader is ready, try these activities. They allow your child to show you what he or she has learned about writing and how much more sophisticated a level of game can be played because of them. After all, word games require the ability to read, write, sort, and sequence—abilities not ordinarily expected in a kindergartner and freshly emerging in your first-grader.

3. WHO AM I?

The activities in this set explore proper nouns and forms of address, and reinforce differentiation skills by encouraging your first-grader not simply to name people, places, and things, but also to describe them.

Your first-grader may already know how to describe himself or herself. He or she may know the family phone number and street address. "On the Street Where You Live," "Draw Your Address," and "Address Book" are designed to help your child learn practical personal information in the course of completing a fun project. At the beginning of the first grade year, your child isn't expected to recite a full home address. By the end of the year, he or she should know the street address—and phone number—at home.

The activities in this set also encourage first-graders to write addresses. This is a fairly advanced activity for most first-graders, and one to encourage in the second and third grades, as well.

4. MEANING-FULL

The activities in this set encourage word recognition and vocabulary development. Play "Invent-a-Word" and "Word Police," then encourage your first-grader to share the games with schoolmates. When your first-grader has begun writing, introduce "Twas Brillig."

5. SOUNDS CRAZY

Bingo is a wonderful game for fun and for learning letters and numbers. A modified version can help your first-grader with phonics, a skill equally important to reading and writing.

Phonics is the topic of the activities in "Sounds Crazy." Your first-grader is probably noisy enough—but direct the noisemaking. It's not simply noise, but an education!

THE NAME GAME

COPY SHOP

Look at the labels on your favorite foods, the titles of your favorite books. You can read the words, right? Give it a try.

Can you find the word milk on the carton, or the word cat on the cover of a book?

Once you can find words, you're ready for "Copy Shop."

You'll need:
tracing paper • a pencil • scissors • tape • index cards • a shoebox with a slot cut into the top

First, find a shoebox or an old cereal box to use as a "copy box." Ask an older person to help you cut a slot into the box. You'll need to be able to open the box, too.

Then, find a word you want to put into the copy machine. Trace the word, using tracing paper and pencil.

Next, rewrite the word onto an index card or trim the tracing paper and tape your traced version of the word onto an index card.

Last, store your word in the copy box.

FOUR-WORD FANTASY

Make up stories using words from your copy box.

> **You'll need:**
> a copy box • a pencil • paper

First, pick four words from your copy box.

Then, think about how those four words could be used to tell one story.

The cat ate the milk and granola from Dad's hat.

Next, write the story. Don't worry about spelling the words that aren't from your "Copy Shop." If you can't write the story by yourself, ask for some help, but be sure to write down your "Copy Shop" words.

Last, give your story a title. Now you're ready to read your story to an audience.

The Cat and the Hat

Once you've mastered "Four-Word Fantasy," try "Five-Word Fantasy." If you want to play in the car, bring your copy box, draw the words, and tell the story out loud rather than writing it down first.

ALPHA DRAW AND ALPHA SNAKE

Use your copy box words for a round of "Alpha Draw."

First, pick three words from your copy box.

Then, put them in A-B-C (alphabetical) order.

When you sort three words easily, pick four words and more to make "Alpha Draw" more challenging. Or, make an "Alpha Snake." Simply continue picking copy box words and fitting them into a running A-B-C sorted row.

APPLE
BONE
CONE
DOG
ELBOW
FROG
GIANT
HOG

SORE THROAT

Pretend you have a sore throat and cannot talk. All you can do is motion with your hands—and write words on paper—to get your message across.

All you'll need for "Sore Throat" is a pencil, paper, and someone willing to play along with you. Who'd have thought a "Sore Throat" could be such fun?

To make "Sore Throat" a double delight, pretend all players have sore throats. You'll all have to write down messages and have them read to be understood.

PEOPLE, PLACES, THINGS, AND ACTIONS

NOUN-SENSE

The words that name people, places, and things are called nouns. Nouns are "naming words." See if you can sort people, places, and things from the picture words below.

S-S-S-S-S-S-S-S: MORE THAN ONE

How do you make a word for a person, place, or thing mean words for people, places, or things?

Usually, you add an -s to the word. It's as easy as that. For example:

pig   pigs
house   houses
car   cars

child

grandmother

policeman

scuba diver

dog

dinosaur

rocket

apple

Or, where a word already ends in s, add -es to the end. For example:

kiss	kisses
glass	glasses
grass	grasses

But there are some exceptions. For example:

mouse	mice
goose	geese
tooth	teeth

store

office

home

school

ACTION WORDS

run

sleep

eat

swim

swing

open

sing

read

buy

watch

kick

cook

PLACES, CAMERA—ACTION!

Some words tell what a person or a thing does. These words are called verbs. Verbs are "action words." Do you know the action words that belong with the pictures below?

ADJECTIVES

Sometimes nouns alone can't create a clear picture. You might say, "Look at the horse," but if there are four horses in the field, you might be asked, "Which horse?"

Adjectives are words that tell about people, places, and things. Adjectives are words that describe.

DIRECTOR'S CHAIR

Once you know a few action words, write them down and take over the "Director's Chair."

You'll need:
index cards • a pencil • actors

First, write down five or more action words on index cards.

Then, convince your friends to be actors in your "action" movie.

Next, direct your actors. Ask each one to draw an index card and act out the action word on the card. You can draw a card, too, and act as well as direct!

MORE SEARCH AND DESTROY

Remember "Search and Destroy" (see p. 19)? Now get ready for "More Search and Destroy."

You'll need:
a copy box • extra index cards • a pencil

First, stack the cards from your copy box into one deck. Then, on extra index cards, make a stack of action word (verb) cards and a stack of words that describe (adjective) cards.

Then, label each stack—noun, verb, adjective.

Many different words are adjectives, including color words:

The <u>brown</u> horse is beautiful.

Number words:

<u>Five</u> children came to my birthday party last year.

And "opposites" words:

The <u>tall</u> kids could see the movie screen but the <u>short</u> kids couldn't.

Next, use the cards to fill in the blanks in the story below.

Once upon a time, there was a _____(noun) with three sons. When he died, he left his sons all that he owned. To the first son, he left the mill. To the second son, he left his _____(adjective) mule. And to the third son, he left his cat.

Now the miller's youngest son was disappointed to be left only a cat. But he soon learned this was no _____(adjective) cat. Why, this cat could _____(verb)!

"Make me a pair of boots," said the cat, "and I'll make you a _____(adjective) man!" And so the youngest son made the cat a pair of boots.

The cat set out in his new boots and hunted _____(noun), which he gathered up to take as a gift to the king. When the cat presented the gift, the King was _____(adjective), indeed. "They're from the Marquis of Carabas," said the cat, and off he went to find his master.

The next day, the king was journeying in his _____(noun) along a roadside near a pond. Bathing in the water was the cat's master. When the cat saw the king approaching, he ran to the roadside and called, "Help, help, thieves have robbed my master, the Marquis of Carabas!" The king remembered the fine gift from the Marquis and ordered his _____(noun) to stop. He then greeted the Marquis and saw he was given a fine suit of _____(noun) and a ride in his carriage.

Meanwhile, the cat ran ahead of the carriage and down the road. He told the farmers in the field that the _____(noun) was coming in a fine _____(adjective) carriage.

"If the king should _____(verb), 'Whose are these fields?',
be certain to _____(verb) that they belong to the Marquis
of Carabas!"

The cat ran ahead until he came to the _____(adjective)
castle of the _____(noun), the very same _____(noun)
who owned the fields.

"I understand you're a very _____(adjective) magician,"
said the cat to the ogre. "Can you make yourself into something
truly _____(adjective)?"

And the ogre did. The cat, frightened a bit, then asked,
"Can you make yourself into something timid and meek?"

Whereupon the ogre turned himself into a _____(adjective) _____(noun) and the cat ate him.

About the same time, the king's carriage approached.
The king had heard from the farmers that the _____(noun)
belonged to the Marquis of Carabas and now they approached
a _____(adjective) castle. There was the cat, bowing to the
_____(noun), and announcing, "Welcome, my master.
Welcome home."

From that day on, the youngest son lived the life of a rich
_____(noun) in his castle with his cat.

Make up your own versions of fairy tales the same way you
"rewrote" "Puss in Boots" above. Simply search and destroy
nouns, verbs, and adjectives from your own storybooks. You
may need a little practice to get going. Once you've played
"More Search and Destroy" with your books, try writing your
own stories, leaving blanks for your friends to choose the nouns,
verbs, and adjectives.

funny

BABY TALK

Use your word cards from "More Search and Destroy" to create sentences. Some of the sentences will sound so silly, you'll think you're talking baby talk.

First, draw an adjective card. Place it on your play area.

Then, draw a noun card. Place it to the right of the adjective card. Next, draw a verb card. Place it to the right of the noun card.

Last, read the cards.

Now, how about asking some silly questions? Follow the instructions for "Baby Talk" above, except draw a verb card, then an adjective card, and, last, the noun card.

WHO AM I?

SPECIAL PEOPLE, PLACES, AND THINGS

Names are special nouns. They start with a capital letter.

What's your name? How do you spell it?

Fred

Helene

Kim

J.P.

Jamal

Erin

Pam

Do you have a pet? What's its name?

Fido
Fluffy
Homer
Fritz
Taffy
Snuggles

What about holidays? They have special names, too.

Thanksgiving
Fourth of July
Valentine's Day
President's Day
Halloween
Columbus Day

SPECIAL DELIVERY! YOUR POSTAL ADDRESS

The U.S. Postal Service uses more than a basic address to get the mail to you. It uses two special types of codes—one for state names and another called zip code.

The *zip code* is the five-digit number that follows most addresses.

The *state* name abbreviation is made up of two capital letters.

J. R. Foster-Lutz
100 West 89th Street
Rabbit Cove, **LA** **12345**

state postal   zip code
abbreviation

The postal abbreviations for the 50 United States are:

AL   Alabama
AK   Alaska
AZ   Arizona
AR   Arkansas
CA   California
CO   Colorado
CT   Connecticut
DE   Delaware
FL   Florida
GA   Georgia
HA   Hawaii
ID   Idaho
IL   Illinois
IN   Indiana
IA   Iowa
KS   Kansas
KY   Kentucky
LA   Louisiana

Guess what? The street or road you live on has a special name, too.

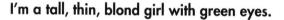

WHAT'S YOUR STORY?

Who are you? You could describe yourself in adjectives and nouns. For example:

I'm a tall, thin, blond girl with green eyes.

I'm a short boy with brown eyes. I wear glasses.

You can describe yourself simply by using your name.

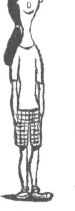

I'm Ariel.   **I'm Francisco.**

CREATE A PAL

No one to play with? Nothing to do? Why not create a pal?

> **You'll need:**
> a pencil • index cards or scrap paper • drawing
> paper • crayons or markers

First, write each of the following words on an individual index
card or piece of scrap paper. These will be your "basic pal" cards.

tall
thin
short
chubby
medium

Then, make a set of "parts" cards that say:

hair
skin
pants
shirt

Next, make a third set of cards with color names on them:

red	blue
brown	purple
yellow	pink
green	orange

PANTS

RED

SHIRT BLUE

Now you're ready to create a pal. First, select a basic pal.

Then, pair off each parts card with a color card.

Next, use crayons or markers to create your pal on drawing paper.

If you're feeling extra ambitious, create a paper doll pal.

You'll need:
construction paper in assorted colors • scissors
• glue or paste • crayons or markers

First, pick people, parts, and color cards as you would for "Create a Pal." Then, instead of drawing your pal, create it out of construction paper.

To create the pal from the cards drawn above, take green construction paper and draw an outline of a tall green body. Then cut out the body.

Next, cut purple construction paper to make hair, red to make pants, and blue to make a shirt. Trace the body piece to make sure the pants and shirt will fit!

Last, glue the hair, pants, and shirt to the body. Now you have a paper doll pal!

ON THE STREET WHERE YOU LIVE

Have you ever invited a new friend over to play who didn't know where you lived? Did you have to tell your friend the name of your street and the number of your house or apartment building?

Have you ever received a letter in the mail? Was it from your grandmother, your uncle, or maybe a pen pal? Did you ever wonder how that letter got to you?

If you can describe where you live, you probably know your address. An address is a special way of describing a person. It's the way you describe where a person lives.

An address has several parts.

NE	Nebraska
NV	Nevada
NH	New Hampshire
NJ	New Jersey
NM	New Mexico
NY	New York
NC	North Carolina
ND	North Dakota
OH	Ohio
OK	Oklahoma
OR	Oregon
PA	Pennsylvania
RI	Rhode Island
SC	South Carolina
SD	South Dakota
TN	Tennessee
TX	Texas
UT	Utah
VT	Vermont
VA	Virginia
WA	Washington
WV	West Virginia
WI	Wisconsin
WY	Wyoming

name

street or road address

J.R. Foster-Lutz
100 West 89th Street
Rabbit Cove LA
12345

city or town

state and zip code

DRAW YOUR ADDRESS

Can you draw your address? Of course you can!

You'll need:
drawing paper • markers

First, draw a picture of you in the middle of your drawing paper. Be sure to leave room for the rest of your "address." Write your name under your picture.

Then, draw the outside of your home behind you. Write your street address underneath.

Next, draw a circle around you and your home. The circle represents your city, town, or rural area. Write your city, town, or area name underneath the circle.

Last, draw the outline of your state around your area circle. If you don't know the shape of your state, just draw a ring around your area circle. Write your state name underneath.

Now you've drawn your address!

ADDRESS BOOK

Once you know how to write your own address, why not keep an address book of other friends and family members?

> **You'll need:**
> a blank address book or a lined notebook or lined notebook paper • staples • a pen or marker

If you're using a premade address book, simply write down addresses of your friends and family members. Most people write the names in alphabetical order by last name. Your address book might have sections already marked "a," "b," "c," and so on.

Arnie Conti
123 Honeysuckle Parkway
Hyacinth, FL 67891

Jenny Davison
456 Rural Highway Number 10
Palm Grove, TX 34567

If you don't have a premade address book, make your own. You can use a plain lined notebook or you can staple together sheets of lined paper to form your address book.

RRRRRRRRRING! THE TELEPHONE

Like addresses, telephone numbers describe where a person can be reached. Although a phone number doesn't describe the location of a home, it does describe a special way a person can be found to talk to.

Do you know your phone number? If not, memorize it now!

Most telephone numbers in the United States are made up of seven numbers. Are there seven in yours?

Then, using pen or marker, write the letters of the alphabet in the upper corners of each page. Don't use a pencil—you want the letters to be bright.

Next, enter the addresses of friends and family. Ask your schoolmates for their addresses and record them in your book. Why not add your friends from camp or sports or religious school, too?

Keep adding names and addresses as you make new friends. Pretty soon, you'll have a full address book.

For an additional feature, ask your friends for their pictures. Paste or staple their pictures in your address book alongside their addresses. You can also include phone numbers in your book.

A LETTER FROM A GALAXY FAR, FAR AWAY

What if a space alien from a different galaxy wanted to write you a letter? Do you know your full address? Below is a complete address to help your alien pen pal send you a note.

J.R. Foster-Lutz
100 W. 89th Street
Rabbit Cove
Louisiana
United States of America
North America
Earth
Solar System
Milky Way

MEANING-FULL

INVENT-A-WORD

Have you ever run out of things to say? You'll never run out again when you play "Invent-a-Word." All you need is a pal and a good imagination!

First, say a word. Words that describe (adjectives) and words for ideas usually work the best. For example, *pretty* or *freedom* work better for "Invent-a-Word" than *doll* or *top*. But any word is okay.

Then, ask your friend to come up with a word that means the same thing. Close is good enough. For example, if you said *pretty,* your friend might say *beautiful*.

Next, it's your turn again. For example, you might say *gorgeous*. Now your pal might say *cute*.

When you can't think of any more words, invent one.

'TWAS BRILLIG . . .

In their nonsense verse and stories, Lewis Carroll and Edward Lear used many made-up words. But some of their words were so descriptive, they are now part of the English language.

Why not try your hand at literature? Just take "Invent-a-Word" a step further.

You'll need:
scrap paper • a pencil • notebook paper

First, play a round of "Invent-a-Word," making sure to write down on scrap paper your invented words and their meanings.

Then, choose a poem or part of a story or play that you like to read. Copy your selection onto notebook paper. Replace all the words you can with words you've invented.

Next, read your story to a friend. Can your friend understand the story—and your invented words?

Rock-a-bye ~~baby,~~ *glebling,*
In the ~~tree~~ *shnarp* top.
When the ~~wind~~ *whooooz* blows
The ~~cradle~~ *crindle* will rock.
When the ~~bough~~ *rem* breaks,
The ~~cradle~~ *crindle* will fall,
And down will come ~~baby~~ *glebling,*
~~Cradle~~ *Crindle* and all.

WORD POLICE

"Word Police" is a scoring game based on "Invent-a-Word." See if you and your friend can fool each other with an invented word. The player who can slip a made-up word past the other gets one point. If a player is on to the made-up word, he or she calls the "Word Police." A player who gets caught by the "Word Police" loses a point. If a player calls the "Word Police" for a false arrest—that is, if the "Word Police" are called but the word is real—the player loses five points.

SOUNDS CRAZY

SOUND BINGO

If you know your letter sounds, you're ready for a round of "Sound Bingo."

You'll need:
26 small pieces of paper or a deck of alphabet cards
• several half sheets of plain paper • pennies (or other small, flat-faced objects)

First, if you don't have a deck of alphabet cards, write each letter on a separate small piece of paper.

Then, make bingo cards. Draw a grid as you would for a game of tic-tac-toe on each half sheet of paper.

Next, write letters in each space. Write the letters in no particular order.

Now, get some friends together and play. Ask someone who knows the letter sounds to be the caller. The rest of the players should each take a bingo card and some markers. Have the caller draw alphabet cards and make each letter sound. Each player who has the letter represented by the letter sound on his or her bingo card puts a marker over that letter. The first player to place three markers in a row wins.

ONOMATOPOEIA

There's a special word for "sound" words. It's onomatopoeia. Following are some examples:

crash
bang
sizzle
hiss
eek
grrrr

Can you think of some more?

ANIMAL NOISES, STREET SOUNDS

Once you know your letter sounds, you can spell the sounds around you. Look at the pictures below. Do the sounds belong?

Now, fill in a sound scene with your own sound words. Imagine a giant ogre. His horrible hairy, green hand is clutching his soup spoon, which he raises to his blubbery lips and slurps down the soup. What sounds is the ogre making? He slurps, he moans, perhaps, his stomach grumbles? What do you think?

Are you ready to draw your own sound scenes?

EASY AS 1, 2, 3...

COUNTING AND MATH SKILLS

At school, your first-grader uses manipulatives—small sets of objects, often tiles—to practice counting and to learn simple addition and subtraction. You can use manipulatives at home, too. Marbles, paper clips, buttons, pasta shells, dried beans—a variety of ordinary things will do.

Give your first-grader a set of 100 items to use as manipulatives. By the end of the first grade year, he or she should master counting to 100 by ones, twos, fives, and tens. Most first-graders are expected to master fact families in addition and subtraction up to 10. If you have a calculator, show your first-grader how to use it.

It's fun to play with and can be used as a self-checking device as well. While your first-grader may master simple column addition and subtraction, he or she will be greatly challenged by messy numbers, or addition and subtraction that involves carrying or regrouping numbers. By using a calculator for messy calculations, your child is encouraged to solve problems that may otherwise be too complex or confusing.

1. KNOW THE NUMBERS

This set of activities focuses on counting games and introduces basic addition and subtraction problems. To play these games, your first-grader should have mastered counting from 1 to 20 and have been introduced to addition by ones.

"Countdown" and "Backwards Hide 'n' Seek" prepare first-graders for subtraction. After all, counting backwards is really subtraction by one.

"The Mark of Melda" and "Pirate Booty" reinforce same-and-different sorting skills as well as counting, addition, and subtraction. If chocolate chip cookies aren't in your child's diet, create several pairs of identical pictures in a few of the pairs. Flash the cards in front of your first-grader and see if he or she can detect which pairs aren't identical and why.

"Advanced Pirate Booty" uses equations to solve the "story problem" inherent in the game. Most first-graders are introduced to equations—both in linear and column formats. Reinforce the school lessons by using equations at home to describe mathematical situations. Often the lessons in a classroom seem abstract and irrelevant if they aren't reinforced in practical situations at home.

"Addition Bingo" challenges your child's basic addition skills, as well as sorting and ordering skills. The game reinforces knowledge of fact families, while encouraging your child to correlate oral instructions with written information.

In the game descriptions, snacks are designated for use as markers on Bingo player cards. The snacks can easily be replaced with buttons, paper clips, pebbles, or other small items.

"Toss\Up Sums" is a math version of "Toss Up Topics" (see page 34), although a certain level of math mastery is required for play of the basic version and variations. Encourage your child to play only when you feel he or she is proficient enough in the math skills to be challenged—rather than frustrated or discouraged—by the snap-and-clap framework. Before you introduce the snap-and-clap sequences, see if your child has fairly quick response time to the "Toss Up Sums" equations.

Remember, the goal by the end of the first grade year is mastery of fact families up to 20, and sequential counting by twos and fives to 100. It's easy to make the "Toss Up Sums" games more difficult—but be sure they're not too difficult when you introduce them to your first-grader.

2. MATH MAPS

"Math Maps" are counting activities that also reinforce spatial skills. As your child masters the basic games, encourage him or her to write equations to describe the maps. For example, from the front door, walk five steps, turn right, walk ten steps, turn right, walk three steps, turn left—and you're in the bathroom. That means $5 + 10 + 3 =$ the number of steps from the front door to the bathroom: $5 + 10 + 3 = 18$.

3. A PLACE FOR EVERYTHING AND EVERYTHING IN ITS PLACE

"Switch-it Digit" and "Add-it Digit" are designed to introduce and reinforce the understanding of place value. Place value is a difficult concept for many primary schoolers. It is a topic taught consistently in the early primary grades.

You can't do too many activities to reinforce the place value concept. Once your first-grader has the basics down, try "Math Table Mystery." It's a place value, counting, and problem-solving activity. Start simply! You can make the game progressively more difficult to keep your first-grader engaged.

"Plus and Minus Puzzles" reinforces your first-grader's understanding of fact families. Once he or she can solve the puzzles, try a variation. Put, for example, ten marbles on the table and count them out loud. Then, have your child close his or her eyes while you take away, say, three marbles. Next, ask your child to count the remaining marbles and immediately tell you how many are missing. It'll take some practice—but it will serve your child well in math classes over the years to come.

4. GET IN SHAPE

By the beginning of first grade, your child should be able to recognize and name several shapes, including: the square, triangle, star, rectangle, and circle. In first grade, more shapes are introduced. The activities in this set reinforce your first-grader's knowledge of shapes and introduce new shapes and geometric patterns.

If you haven't the inclination to sew a patterned quilt, alter the activity to a cut-and-paste construction paper game. The "quilt" squares can be glued to poster board.

KNOW THE NUMBERS

COUNTDOWN

It's shuttle liftoff day and you're in the control tower . . .

20, 19, 18, 17, 16

Engines . . .

15, 14, 13, 12, 11

Ignition . . .

10, 9, 8, 7, 6, 5, 4, 3, 2, 1

Liftoff!

Congratulations, flight engineer. You've passed the test. Now you're ready for the real countdown. Can you count backward from 20 without any help?

REWIND HIDE 'N' SEEK

Have you ever seen a videotape run backward? The action in reverse can look pretty funny. But you don't need videotape for the laugh. Just try a game of "Rewind Hide 'n' Seek." You can play with one friend or several, indoors or out.

First, play a real game of hide 'n' seek. Decide who's "it." While "it" stands in the safe zone and counts to 20, the other players hide. Then "it" tries to catch the players before they come out of hiding and touch the safe zone.

Now, when "it" yells "freeze" when he or she captures a player, all the players stop where they are.

Next, "it" yells "rewind" and all the players move backward as if rewinding the game. "Rewind Hide 'n' Seek" ends when "it" finishes counting in the safe zone—backward from 20 to 1.

Why not videotape a game or two?

THE MARK OF MELDA

Who is Melda? Where will she strike? What? She's already been here!

Make some special chocolate chip cookies. Then enjoy a treat while you see if you can fool your friends or if they can find "The Mark of Melda."

> **You'll need:**
> **chocolate chip cookie dough** • **candy-coated chocolate or peanut butter candies**

First, prepare cookies according to the recipe.

Then, slip in "The Mark of Melda"—a special piece of coated candy.

PIRATE BOOTY

Arrrrrrrr, me buckos. Shiver me timbers! Who's got the treasure, who's got dross?

Who's the richest pirate on the seven seas? Next time you have a party, play a little "Pirate Booty" and see who's golden and who's not.

You'll need:
treasure (gold foil-wrapped chocolate coins, pennies, pretty stones, small candies, or play jewelry) • dross (washers, bolts, paper clips, etc.) • 8 to 10 lunch-size paper bags

First, prepare booty bags. Divide treasure and booty randomly into paper bags. You want a different amount of treasure and booty in each bag!

Then, ask a grown-up to hide the bags.

Next, call the pirates together and tell them to begin searching the seven seas for booty. Once all the booty bags have been found, have each pirate separate the treasure from the dross.

Last, let the pirates count their pieces of treasure and their pieces of dross. The pirate with the most treasure wins. The pirate with the most dross walks the plank!

SIMPLIFIED PIRATE BOOTY

If both sorting and counting seem a little difficult, make "Pirate Booty" a simple counting game. All you have to do is eliminate the dross from the treasure bags. You can also make "Pirate Booty" a simple sorting game. Just eliminate counting the treasure and dross pieces.

ADVANCED PIRATE BOOTY

Now, if you're a sporting buccaneer, you might want to take "Pirate Booty" a yard arm—or two—further.

Variation A: Pirates count up the number of treasures pieces, then the number of dross. Pirates then take away the number of dross pieces from the number of treasure pieces.

The pirate with the greatest remainder wins.

Variation B: Treasure pieces are worth ten points each. Pirates total up their treasure counting by ten. Dross is counted as five minus points each. Pirates total up their dross by counting by five. Then pirates take away the number of dross points from the treasure points to find a total.

ADDITION BINGO

Here's a delicious version of Bingo, Win, lose-
and munch!

First, make your Bingo player cards. Cut sheets of construction in
half to make two player cards measuring about 4 by 5 1/2 inches.
Cut enough sheets to allow one player card per player.

Then, using a non-toxic marker and a ruler, draw a grid on
each player card. The grid should consist of five rows across
and five columns down. Be sure to leave a sixth row across
the top for headings.

Finish creating the player cards by heading
each column *A, B, C, D,* and *E.*
Write the numbers *1* to *20*
randomly in the squares below
the headings.

Then, on each index card, write *A*, *B*, *C*, *D*, and *E* and an addition sentence for any fact family with a sum from *1* to *20*. Use all the following combinations:

0+20	7+13	14+6
1+19	8+12	15+5
2+18	9+11	16+4
3+17	10+10	17+3
4+16	11+9	18+2
5+15	12+8	19+1
6+14	13+7	20+0

Next, shuffle the index cards and place them face down in front of the caller. Distribute player cards to each player along with a cup full of snacks.

Last, play Bingo. The caller draws cards one at a time and reads the letter and math sentence aloud. Players add the numbers and check the letter row on their player cards for the sum. If the sum is on the player card, players mark it with a snack. When a row or column on a player's card is completely marked with snacks, the player calls, "Bingo!" Then, win or lose, all players eat the snacks from their cards and play again.

TOSS UP SUMS

Have you played "Toss Up Topics" (see p. 34)? Here's a number version that will challenge your addition skills.

First, learn the "Toss Up Sums" jingle:

Toss Up Sums,
Time to have some fun,
Toss Up adding now begins,
So answer the equation.

Then, learn the jingle with the snap-and-clap sequence.

Toss [clap knees] **Up** [clap hands] **Sums** [snap twice],
Time to [clap knees] **have some** [clap hands] **fun** [snap twice],
Toss Up [clap knees] **adding** [clap hands] **now** [snap once]
begins,[snap twice].
So answer [clap knees] **the** [clap hands] **equation** [snap twice].

Next, play begins. All players recite the jingle with the clap-and-snap sequence. The first player then recites an equation, within one snap-and-clap sequence. The next player says the sum with the next snap-and-clap sequence. Continue to play until an equation or sum is missed within a sequence. The player who misses is out of the game and a new round begins.

A variation on "Toss Up Sums" is "Toss Up Take Away," a subtraction game. Play proceeds as in "Toss Up Sums," although the jingle is somewhat different:

Toss Up Take Away,
Subtracting numbers fills the day.
Toss Up Take Away begins
Starting with the numbers.

From another variation, play a sequential counting game within a snap-and-clap sequence. Use a different jingle:

Counting, counting 1, 2, 3,
That's too easy, can't you see?
Count instead by twos or threes,
Or by the number named by me.

Within the next snap-and-clap sequence, the first player names the number for sequential counting, for example, two. The next player says the first number of the sequence, for example, four. Play continues, for example, the next player says six, the next, eight, and so on, until a player misses.

MATH MAPS

Bedtime! Take out the garbage, please! Walk the dog, dear! When you have to go someplace or do something you don't want to do, make a game of it.

At bedtime, count the steps you take from the kitchen to the bathroom to brush your teeth. Then count the steps from the bathroom to your bed. Tomorrow night, make the trip in giant steps. How many steps did you take? The next night, try baby steps.

How many steps does it take to get from the back door to the garbage bins? What if you walk in a straight line across the grass? Now, how many steps does it take if you follow the sidewalk to the driveway, then down to the bins?

Suppose it takes 10 steps from your bedroom to the dog's bed, another 6 steps to the door, 30 to the elevator, and 45 from the lobby floor out to the garden. How many total steps does it take to bring Fluffy out for a walk?

10 + 6 + 30 + 45

Make counting easier with a simple variation. Carry a calculator with you as you pace off your math maps. Enter each number of steps from destination to destination, add them, and at the end of your route, total them up!

Why not make a math map of your house, playground, zoo, or another favorite place?

You'll need:
scratch paper or graph paper • a pencil • poster board • markers

First, using scratch paper and a pencil, make notes for your map. If you're mapping the playground, sketch the location of the swing set, the play area, the sandbox, teeter-totters, and other equipment. Then, starting at your favorite spot—for example, the swing set—count the number of steps between the swing set and the sandbox. Then count off the number of steps between the sandbox and the play area, and so on, until you've counted off the distances between all the major playground locations.

Then, at home, use your sketch and notes to recreate the playground on poster board. Draw, for example, the swing set.

Next, sketch stepping stones or squares to represent the number of steps to the next piece of equipment you want to draw. You could also use graph paper.

Finish drawing all locations on your map, showing them with stepping stones in between.

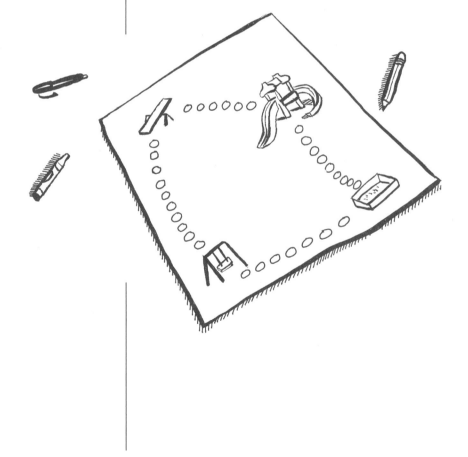

MAP GAME

Math maps make nice posters—and even better game boards. Get a friend to play with, some dice, or a deck of cards, and see who makes it through the math map first.

You'll need:
a math map • dice or playing cards (number cards only)
• playing pieces (different coins, paper clips, etc.)

First, decide where to begin the game on the map and where to finish. Put your markers at the beginning.

Then, roll dice or draw number cards to see how many steps you can move along the stepping stones.

Each player takes a turn and play moves along until a player reaches the finish line.

A PLACE FOR EVERYTHING & EVERYTHING IN ITS PLACE

SWITCH-IT DIGIT, ADD-IT DIGIT

Have you ever noticed that we really have only ten symbols, called numerals or digits, for writing numbers? They are:

0, 1, 2, 3, 4, 5, 6, 7, 8, and 9

All our numbers are combinations of those ten digits.

So, if a number is written with more than one digit, the order of the digits is pretty important, right? Let's see . . .

What happens if you switch the digits in 15?

15
51

You get 51!

Are you ready for a game of "Switch-it Digit?"

> **You'll need:**
> **10 index cards • a marker**

First, write one of each of the following numbers on each index card: **10, 11, 12, 13, 14, 15, 16, 17, 18,** and **19**.

Then, on the back of each index card, switch the digits from the number on the front and write the Switch-it Digit number. For example, on the back of the **12** card, write **21.**

Next, test yourself. Flash each card in front of your eyes. Then say, as quickly as you can, the "Switch-it Digit." Check by turning the card over.

You can play "Switch-it Digit" with your friends, too. See who can switch-it fastest.

Once you've mastered "Switch-it Digit" with **10** to **19,** add more cards to your deck until you have **90** or more.

So what is "Add-it Digit?" It's a digit addition flashcard game that might make you twitch-it—at least, at first.

> **You'll need:**
> index cards • a marker

PLACE VALUE

The value of a numeral depends on where it's located in a number. 1 is worth 1 in the following numbers:

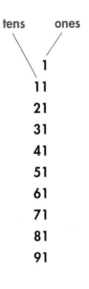

tens   ones

1
11
21
31
41
51
61
71
81
91

That's because 1 is in the ones place in each of the numbers.

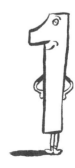

But 1 is worth 10 in the following numbers:

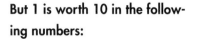
tens   ones

10
11
12
13
14
15
16
17
18
19

That's because 1 is in the tens place in those numbers.

First, write numbers on the front of each index card as you did for "Switch-it Digit."

Then, on the back of each card, write the sum of the digits on the front. For example, on the back of the **14** card, write **5** because **1 + 4 = 5.**

Next, test yourself. See how quickly you can come up with the "Add-it Digit" sum.

Like "Switch-it Digit," try a round with your friends. When you master the first set of numbers, add "Add-it Digit" cards to your deck.

MATH TABLE MYSTERY

Solve math table mysteries.

First, find an addition table or make one on a sheet of paper. Be sure you have enough room on each number square to fit a playing piece. It should look like this:

Make several copies of the addition table to use as game cards.

Then, make your instruction cards. You'll need help with these. Here are some examples to follow:

A. My number has two digits. One of my digits is a 3. I'm in the fifth row. What number am I?

B. I'm a number less than 50, but greater than 20.
One of my digits is 7.
My other digit is 4.
What number am I?

C. I have a 5 in my tens place.
My other digit is less than 7 but greater than 1.
The digit is equal to the value of my tens place minus 3.
What number am I?

Think up some more instructions, and write them down, too.

Next, gather some players together and give each one a game card and a playing piece.

Last, follow the instructions. See who solves the mystery by placing the playing piece on the correct number on the game card.

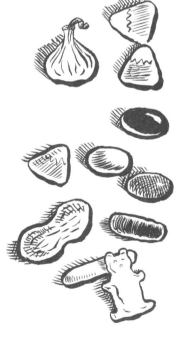

A SWEETER VERSION

Use candies as playing pieces when you play "Math Table Mystery" for a sweeter version of the game. When you've solved a mystery, eat your playing piece. Get another candy and play again!

Answers to "Math Table Mysteries:" A.43 B.47 C.52

PLUS AND MINUS PUZZLES

Have you learned about fact families? They're groups of numbers that belong together in addition and subtraction. For example:

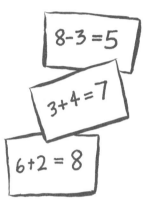

2 + 2 = 4 and 4 - 2 = 2   **2, 2 and 4 form a fact family**

3 + 2 = 5 and 5 - 2 = 3   **2, 3 and 5 form a fact family**

You can make fact family puzzles and solve them with your friends. When you've had some practice, see who can solve the puzzles fastest.

You'll need:
scratch paper • a pencil • half a sheet of paper
• a marker

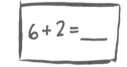

First, write down ten or more fact families.

Then, erase one number from each equation in each fact family.

Next, copy each fact family—with the missing number—onto its own half sheet of paper.

Now, you're ready to play. Flash each fact family sheet and see who can solve the puzzle.

NUMERICAL ASSOCIATIONS

GET IN SHAPE

NAME YOUR SHAPES

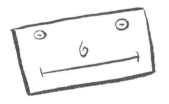

SHAPE COLLECTOR

Look at the shapes (at left and right). Do you know their names?

circle, square, rectangle, triangle, parallelogram, star, trapezoid, pentagon, hexagon

STRETCHED OUT

Triangles always have three sides. But some can look kind of strange . . .

Quadrilaterals always have four sides, but they can look even stranger!

You can make some weird triangles and quadrilaterals with some simple tools.

First, start with triangles. Push three pins into the wallboard.

Then, wrap a rubber band around the outside of the push pins.

Next, move the push pins around and see how the triangle changes.

Use four push pins to make quadrilaterals.

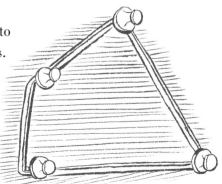

CHANGING SHAPE

Can you take one shape and change it into another? Sure. Follow along.

You'll need:
construction paper • a pencil • a ruler • scissors

First, using a ruler and a pencil, draw a square, a triangle, and a rectangle. If you can, draw a pentagon (five sides) and a hexagon (six sides), too.

Then, cut them out.

Next, cut the shapes as shown. Now you have a whole new set of shapes.

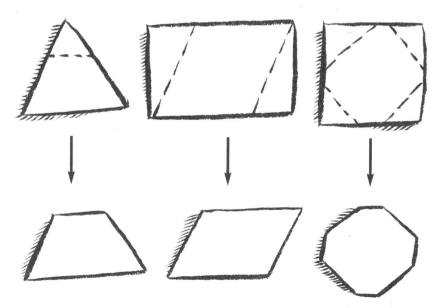

PATTERN PIECES, PATTERN QUILT

Use shapes to make patterns for quilts! How? Read on.

You'll need:
felt squares • fabric scraps • trim scraps • glue
• thread and needle

First, cut fabric scraps into shapes.

Then, arrange the shapes to create a design on a felt square.

Next, glue the shapes in place. Decorate with trim, if you wish.

Make several squares. You can make
the same pattern on each square,
or make a new pattern each time.
When you've made several squares,
lay them out into a rectangle.
Get some help and sew
them together into your
very own quilt.

IT'S ABOUT TIME, MONEY, AND MEASUREMENT

TIME, MONEY, AND MEASUREMENT

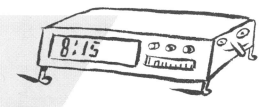

OVERVIEW FOR PARENTS

By the end of the first grade year, many children recognize and understand the basics of measuring time and length and counting money. These are difficult concepts, however, and are taught, reviewed, expanded upon, and reinforced throughout the early primary years.

Without practice, many first-graders lose the time, money, and measurement concepts they tenuously grasped in school lessons. But these are practical concepts, useful in virtually every real-life circumstance. So involve your child in your own timekeeping, in simple money transactions, and in measuring household items. By connecting these difficult concepts to everyday events, your child becomes more curious and eager to tackle these challenges.

As a guideline, encourage your first-grader to know time to half hours and to know the days of the week and the months in order. Introduce the idea of seasons and the months they occupy, although don't expect mastery here. Also, help your child use a calendar, but, again, don't expect mastery.

Most first-graders know the names of coins by year's end and recognize one- and five-dollar bills. Usually, they are asked to measure to the half inch, and to measure by centimeter.

Encourage your child to measure things at home. Can the sofa fit through the door? Measure both and see. You don't have to use inches to measure, however. Try introducing nonstandard measures—say, fork lengths, or penny widths. These nonstandard measures help your child correlate the idea of units and stated measures. If your child hears, "It's three long," you'll want him or her to know to ask, "Three what?"

1. THE TIME OF DAY

"The Time of Day" reinforces basic ideas about time and its passage by encouraging your child to use critical thinking skills to solve time-telling problems. The activity set shows how time can be measured without using clocks or calendars, and introduces some alternative time-telling techniques.

2. TICK TOCK

This set of activities reviews how clocks—both analog and digital—display time. It also applies time-telling to real life situations, including schedules and timetables. A potent incentive for your child to learn to tell time is the promise of knowing when a favorite program is on television, when a special play or concert starts, or when a birthday party or special event is scheduled.

3. THE COURSE OF TIME

The passage of time over weeks, months, and years is reinforced in this set of activities. Although it's difficult for a first-grader to comprehend time frames as distant as months or years, he or she nevertheless can measure off the passage of time and become more familiar with the length of a day, week, and month.

4. SPARE CHANGE

Counting money is reviewed and new coins are introduced in this set of activities. Real-life applications for counting money are also suggested to help your child relate money to its purpose.

5. HOW LONG?

These activities encourage measuring—indoors and out! Encourage your child to measure anything and everything within reason. It's excellent practice and sharpens spatial skills. You may want to invest in a child's measuring tape. It makes a great toy—and tremendous learning tool!

Also, encourage your child to take nontraditional measures. For example, measure the distance around the kitchen in soup ladles, or the length of the daily newspaper in paper clips.

THE TIME OF DAY

ANCIENT TIME

Long before the clocks we use today were even invented, people were measuring time. Some early timepieces used the sun's light. If a day was rainy or gray, the clocks were useless. Other clocks used sand grains, water, and even candle wax to show time passing.

Shadow sticks are simply sticks stuck straight up in the ground. Time is told by looking at the length of the shadow that is cast from a stick.

S ome days seems longer than others. They go so slowly you can hardly wait for something to happen. Other days fly by. It seems it's bedtime right when you're having the most fun of all! But all days are made up of the same number of hours. That's right! There are 24 hours in every day.

So how can you tell what part of the day you're in? One way is to think about things that happen every day, things like breakfast, lunch, and dinner.

evening   **morning**   **midday**

Match the time of day to the meals shown above. You know breakfast happens in the morning, lunch is eaten at midday, and dinner is served in the evening.

The sun can also help you keep track of time. Where is the sun in the sky when you first wake up? Where is it right about lunchtime? And where's the sun when you climb into bed for a good night's sleep?

Sundials are really shadow sticks, but with some special additions. The sticks are called gnomons. The gnomon is set on a clock face with numbers scratched into it. The time of day is read by following the shadow to the number on the face.

sunrise	morning	noon
afternoon	**evening**	**sunset**

Match the time of day to the pictures of the sun. Noon is when the sun is at its highest point in the sky. At noon, your toys, your house, the neighbor's tree, and the dog won't cast much of a shadow.

Water clocks were used more than 3,000 years ago in ancient Egypt. These clocks were called clepsydras. Time was measured by the level of water in the bowl. The more water, the more time that has passed.

TIMETELLER'S MATCH GAME

You've seen how mealtimes and the sun can be used as time-pieces—things used to figure out the time. Can you think of some other timepieces? If you can, you can create a timeteller's match game or a timeteller's museum.

You'll need:
scrap paper • a pencil • drawing paper
• crayons or markers

Sandglasses are hundreds of years old—but are still used today! You might even have a small sandglass, called an egg-timer, in your kitchen. Sandglasses have two bowl-like chambers joined by a narrow tube. One chamber is filled with sand. When the glass is turned so the sand is in the upper chamber, the sand slowly falls, grain by grain, into the lower chamber. In some large sandglasses, called hourglasses, it takes 60 minutes (or one hour) for the sand to fall from the upper chamber to the lower chamber.

Think of three or more different timepieces. Write them down on your scrap paper so you remember your ideas.

If you're creating a match game, draw pictures of the timepieces you wrote down on your list. Try to show in your picture how the timepieces help tell the time. For some timepieces, you may want to draw more than one picture.

Then, write labels for each of your timepieces.

Next, paste down your timepiece picture on one side of a large piece of drawing paper. Paste the labels on the other side. Be sure the labels don't line up with their pictures.

Last, find a pal to play the match game. Ask your friend to match the labels to the timepiece pictures.

TIMETELLER'S MUSEUM

You can create a timepiece museum in your bedroom, backyard, or garage. Just be sure your parents know what you're up to. (You don't want to set up your museum on the day your dad is painting the ceiling in your museum space!) Remember, making a museum is hard work. You might want to do this activity with a friend or two.

> **You'll need:**
> scrap paper • a pencil • drawing paper • sample timepieces • a display area to show your timepieces

Candle clocks show how time has passed by showing the amount of wax burned away from the candle. The shorter the candle becomes, the more time has passed.

To create the museum, find the objects that make up the timepieces you listed on your scrap paper. If you don't have the real objects, make them out of toys or other things you find around the house or in the garage. (For example, you couldn't put the sun in your museum. But you could use a ball to stand for the sun in your display.) Just don't take objects that aren't yours without asking permission! Then put your timepieces together in museum-type displays.

Next, write labels for each display in your museum. Place the labels near each display.

Last, invite the neighbor kids and even their parents to visit the timepiece museum.

TICK TOCK

MODERN CLOCKS

Today, we use clocks to tell the exact time of day. A day is measured in hours. Each day is 24 hours long.

12 a.m.

3 a.m.

6 a.m.

9 a.m.

12 p.m.

3 p.m.

6 p.m.

9 p.m.

Hours are divided into minutes. Each hour is 60 minutes long.

Look at the clocks below. They are called analog clocks. They have a circular face. The face is divided into 12 main parts and 60 smaller parts. The 12 main parts show the hours in the day. The little arrow, or "hand," points to the hour and shows one hour passing into the next. The 60 smaller parts show the minutes within each hour. The big hand points to the minutes.

Look at these clocks without faces. There are no big or little hands to measure the minutes and hours. Instead, the hour is shown in the first number, the minutes in the second. The hours and minutes are separated by the **:**. These clocks are called digital clocks.

Can you decide which of the clocks below show the same time?

PRACTICE CLOCK

Learn to tell time with your very own practice clock.

You'll need:
a paper plate • construction paper • scissors
• a paper clasp • a marker

First, divide the paper plate into 12 "hours" and write the numbers as shown.

Then, cut a big hand and a little hand out of construction paper.

Next, secure the hands to the clock face by clasping them in the center of the plate.

Now you're ready to play with time!

RAILWAY STATION

Use your practice clock to play "Railway Station." You're the stationmaster. You must schedule the day's trains.

You'll need:
poster board • a yard stick • a marker
• a practice clock

First, draw a line down the poster board to make three columns. The two columns on the left should be narrower than the column on the right. Label the columns "Departure Time," "Track," and "Destination."

Then, draw five to ten rows across the poster board. Now you've got a schedule board.

Next, fill in the train schedule on the schedule board. Write the time the train will be leaving the station in the "Departure Time" column, a number between one and ten in the "Track" column, and the name of a nearby town in the "Destination" column.

Last, use your practice clock to show the time at the railway station. Turn the clock to match departure time. Then announce, "All aboard. The 10:30 train to Honeydale is now boarding on Track 3. All aboard!"

SHOWTIME

Use your practice clock as part of other activities. For example, if you're putting on a play (see p. 31), use your practice clock as a theater clock. "Curtain is at 8!"

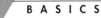

THE COURSE OF TIME

Clocks measure the time of day. Calendars measure the time over longer periods. Calendars are divided into weeks, months, and years. There are 7 days in a week, 28 to 31 days in a month, and 12 months in a year.

The following words are the names of the months and weekdays. They're all mixed up. Can you tell the names of the weekdays from the names of the months?

March	**Thursday**
Tuesday	**April**
December	**Saturday**
August	**May**
Friday	**February**
January	**June**
Wednesday	**October**
November	Monday
Sunday	**July**
September	

Now look again. The days of the week are printed in color and the days of the month are printed in black.

PERPETUAL CALENDAR

You can make a calendar that's good every week, every month, and every year. It's called a perpetual calendar. Perpetual means always.

You'll need:
poster board • index cards • markers • a yardstick • adhesive Velcro™ dots • a shoe box

First, make a grid on the poster board. Leave a border across the top and include 7 columns and 5 rows in the grid. Label each column, from left to right, Sunday, Monday, Tuesday, and so on.

Then, label index cards with the names of the months and with numbers from 1 to 31.

Next, attach the stiff side of adhesive Velcro™ dots to each box in the grid below the border. Place the stiff side of one more Velcro™ dot in the center of the border.

Attach the fuzzy side of adhesive Velcro™ dots to all the month name cards and day number cards. Consult a calendar and stick the numbers in the appropriate places. Put the month name in the center of the border.

Last, hang your perpetual calendar on a wall. Change it each month. Store unused number and month name cards in a shoebox.

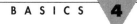

SPARE CHANGE

Counting money is a valuable skill. When you know how to count money and swap change, you'll be ready to set up shop. For example, you could set up a lemonade stand or charge admission to your puppet theater. You might even have a toy tag sale along with the family garage sale. But you can't buy and sell until you know your coins and bills!

WHAT'S IT WORTH?

Look at the pictures below. Do you know what they're called? Do you know what they're worth?

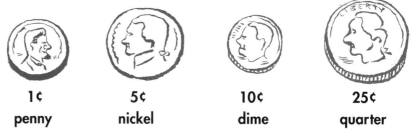

1¢	5¢	10¢	25¢
penny	nickel	dime	quarter

What about paper money? Do you know your bills?

$1.00	$5.00	$10.00	$20.00
one dollar	five dollars	ten dollars	twenty dollars

FAIR TRADE

When is five for one a fair deal? When it's five pennies for a nickel. But, beware! Five nickels for a penny is not a fair deal. Do you know why? If you don't, play a few rounds of "Fair Trade" with someone in the know and you'll soon be set straight.

You'll need:
300 pennies • 4 quarters • 10 dimes • 20 nickels

First, take the all the coins—except for the pennies. The other player is the banker and holds all the pennies.

Then, ask the banker for pennies. For example, you may offer the banker a dime and ask for 10 pennies. Be sure you name your coin and ask for a fair trade.

Next, trade in another coin, and another until the banker is out of pennies. If you counted correctly, you should have all the pennies and the banker all the coins at the end of the round.

Now it's your turn to be the banker. Be careful! You never know when someone'll ask for 10 pennies for a nickel!

THE PRICE IS RIGHT

Practice counting money by setting up a pretend store.

You'll need:
toys, collectors cards, play clothes, or other things to sell
• price tags • a marker • a shoe box • 4 small
paper cups • play money or spare coins and bills

First, assemble the items you want to tag for sale in your pretend store.

Then put price tags on each item and mark the amount each will cost. You can make price tags out of construction paper and string.

Next, make a shoebox into a cash register for your store. Separate paper money and put it on one side of the box. Then, place the four paper cups in the other side of the box. Put pennies in one cup, nickels in another, dimes in the third, and quarters in the last. Be sure to set aside some money for customers to use!

Last, open your store—and make change, change, change!

TICKETS!

Sell tickets to your theatrical productions (for example, see p. 31) at your very own box office.

> **You'll need:**
> construction paper • scissors • a marker • a cash box • play money or spare coins and bills • a box office

First, cut tickets out of construction paper. You can decorate them on one side with a marker, write "admit one," or both.

Then, assemble your cash box. Follow the instructions for "The Price Is Right."

Next, sell your tickets to all customers and invite them to your show. Curtain up!

BUILD A BOX OFFICE

Use a card table or a snack tray as your box office, or make a booth out of an oversized box. Cut a window in one side of the box and a door in the opposite side. Install a snack tray and you're all set!

If you put a curtain over the window, you'll have a great puppet theater!

HOW LONG?

MEASURING TOOLS

Before rulers and yardsticks, people used everything from grain to belts to body parts to measure length and distance.

digit - width of an adult finger

finger - three grains of barley laid end to end (about the length of an adult finger)

hand - length of an adult hand, from wrist to tip of middle finger

foot - length of an adult man's foot

yard - three Roman feet

fathom - distance between hands on two outstretched arms

INCH WORM

How do the things around you measure up? Measure them and see!

You'll need:
a tape measure or a 4- to 6-foot piece of rope with inches marked on it

First, get a tape measure. If you don't have one, get a piece of rope. Use a yardstick or ruler to mark inches along the rope. Now you're ready to measure.

Next, choose two things to measure and compare. Why not start with your height and the distance around your waist? Or use your rope to measure the distance from your front door to the refrigerator and the front door to the television. Or measure the height of a tabletop and the length of the tabletop. Once you get started, you'll be hard to stop!

Which is longer? Which is wider? Which is farther?

INVENT A RULER

You don't need rulers and tape measures to measure. You can use anything. For example, you can measure the length of your foot in pennies, The width of the sidewalk in ice pop sticks, and the width of a table in soup cans.

If you want to change your invented measure into inches, use a ruler or tape to measure your measuring tool. For example, your ice pop stick may measure 5 inches. If the sidewalk is 6 ice pop sticks wide, you can add to find the sidewalk width in inches:

$$5 + 5 + 5 + 5 + 5 + 5 = 30$$

MEASURE YOUR MATH MAPS

Remember "Math Maps" (see p. 85)? Why not use your measuring tools to make your math maps. By the way, the pace—the distance covered in a single step—was a standard measure in ancient Egypt. Have you ever heard the expression "pacing off"? That's just what you did to make your maps—you paced off the distance between one area and another.

span - width of an outstretched adult hand, from thumb to pinky

cubit - length from the elbow to tip of the middle finger on an adult man

pace - distance of a step from the heel of the back foot to the toe of the front foot

mile - 1,000 paces

rod - length covered by the left feet of 16 men, lined up heel to toe

GOOD BOOKS TO READ

Aardema, Verna. *Princess Gorilla and a New Kind Of Water*. (New York: Dial Books for Young Readers, 1988).

Adler, David. *The Fourth Floor Twins Series*. (New York: Viking Kestrel, 1988).

Adler, David. *The Cam Jansen Series and the Mystery of the Stolen Diamonds*. (New York: Viking Press, 1978).

Alderson, Ida: *The Wool Smugglers*. (New York: Margaret K. McElderry Books, 1987).

Aliki. *Dinosaur Bones*. (New York: Crowell, 1988).

Aliki. *Dinosaurs Are Different*. (New York: Crowell, 1985).

Aliki. *Digging Up Dinosaurs*. (New York: Crowell, 1981).

Asch, Frank. *Just Like Daddy*. (New York: Simon & Schuster, 1981).

Atwater, Richard and Florence. *Mr. Popper's Penguins*. (New York: Scholastic, 1969).

Bang, Molly. *Wiley and The Hairy Man*. (New York: Macmillan, 1976).

Bang, Molly. *Ten, Nine, Eight*. (New York: Greenwillow Books, 1983).

Barton, Byron. *Dinosaurs, Dinosaurs*. (New York: Crowell, 1989).

Bayer, Jane E. *My Name Is Alice.* (New York: Dial Books for Young Readers, 1984).

Benchley, Nathaniel, illustrated by Arnold Lobel. *Sam the Minuteman.* (New York: Harper Audio, 1990).

Berenstain, Stan. *Old Hat, New Hat.* (New York: Random House, 1970).

Berenstain, Stan. *Bears in the Night.* (New York: Random House, 1971).

Blake, Quentin. *Mrs. Armitage on Wheels.* (New York: Knopf/Random House, 1989).

Blocksma, Mary. *Rub-a-Dub-Dub: What's in the Tub?* (Chicago: Children's Press, 1984).

Blume, Judy. *Freckle Juice.* (New York: Four Winds Press/Macmillan, 1971).

Bond, Michael, illustrated by Peggy Fortnum. *A Bear Called Paddington.* (New York: Dell, 1958).

Bonsall, Crosby Barbara Newell. *And I Mean It, Stanley.* (New York: Harper & Row, 1974).

Bonsall, Crosby Barbara Newell. *The Day I Had to Play with My Sister.* (New York: Harper & Row, 1972).

Bonsall, Crosby Barbara Newell. *Mine's the Best.* (New York: Harper & Row, 1973).

Brandt, Betty. *Special Delivery.* (Washington D. C.: Carol, 1988).

Brown, Ruth. *A Dark, Dark Tale.* (New York: Dial, 1981).

Bulla, Clyde Robert, illustrated by Thomas B. Allen. *The Chalk Box Kid.* (New York: Random House, 1987).

Burgess, Thornton W., illustrated by Harrison Cady. *Old Mother West Wind.* (New York: Grosset & Dunlap, 1988).

Burgess, Thornton. *Adventures of Series: Old Man Coyote.* (New York: Grosset & Dunlap, 1944).

Burmingham, John. *The School.* (New York: The Doherty Associates, 1990).

Calhoun, Mary. *Jack and the Whoopee Wind.* (New York: Morrow, 1987).

Cameron, Ann, illustrated by Ann Strugnell. *The Stories Julian Tells.* (New York: Knopf, 1986).

Cameron, Ann. *Julian's Glorious Summer.* (New York: Random House, 1987).

Carter, David. *How Many Bugs in a Box?* (Boston: Dorling Kindersley/ Houghton Mifflin Company, 1992).

Caudill, Rebecca, illustrated by Nancy Grossman. *Did You Carry The Flag Today, Charley?* (New York: Holt, Rinehart & Winston, 1966).

Cerf, Bennett. *Bennett Cerf's Book of Animal Riddles.* (New York: Beginner Books, 1964).

Cole, Joanna. *Bony-Legs.* (New York: Four Winds Press, 1983).

Cole, Joanna. *The Magic School Bus at the Water Works.* (New York: Scholastic Inc., 1986).

Conford, Ellen. *Can Do, Jenny Archer.* (Boston: Springboard Books, 1991).

Cresswell, Helen. *Trouble.* (New York: Dutton, 1987).

Crews, Donald. *Flying.* (New York: Greenwillow Books, 1986).

Dee, Ruby. *Two Ways to Count to Ten.* (New York: Henry Holt, 1988).

De La Mare, Walter. *Molly Whuppie.* (New York: Knopf, 1957).

De La Mare, Walter, illustrated by Elinore Blaisedell. *Rhymes and Verses: Collected Poems for Young People.* (New York: Knopf, 1957).

De Paola, Tomie. *Fin M'Coul: The Giant of Knockmany Hill.* (New York: Holiday House, 1981).

De Paola, Tomie. *The Legend of The Indian Paintbrush.* (New York: Putnam, 1988).

De Regnier, Beatrice Schenk (Freedman). *Jack the Giant-Killer.* (New York: Atheneum, 1987).

Dr. Seuss. *Green Eggs and Ham.* (New York: Beginner Books/Random House, 1960).

Dr. Seuss. *One Fish, Two Fish, Red Fish, Blue Fish.* (New York: Beginner Books/Random House, 1960).

Dr. Seuss. *The Cat in the Hat.* (New York: Random House, 1957).

Eastman, Philip D. *Are You My Mother?* (New York: Beginner Books; P.D. Eastman).

Eastman, Philip D. *Go, Dog, Go!* (New York: Beginner Books, 1989).

Elliott, Dan, illustrated by Norman Chartier. *Grover Learns to Read.* (New York: Random House, Children's Television Workshop, 1982).

Fleischman, *The Scarebird.* (New York: Greenwillow Books, 1988).

Fritz, Jean, illustrated by Margot Tomes. *And Then What Happened, Paul Revere?* (New York: Coward, McCann & Geoghegan, 1973).

Gannett, Ruth Stiles, illustrated by Ruth Chrisman Gannett. *My Father's Dragon.* (New York: Random House, 1948).

Giff. *Ronald Morgan Goes to Bat.* (New York: Viking Kestrel, 1988).

Ginsburg, Mirra. *The Chick and the Duckling.* (New York: Macmillan Co., 1972).

Goble, Paul. *Iktomi and the Boulder.* (New York: Orchard Books, 1988).

Greenwald, Sheila. *Give Us a Great Big Smile, Rosy Cole.* (Boston: Little, Brown, 1981).

Gryski, Camilla. *Cat's Cradle, Owl's Eyes: A Book of String Games.* (New York: William Morrow, 1984).

Harrison, David L. *Wake Up, Sun.* (Chicago: Reilly & Lee Books, 1970).

Haywood, Carolyn. *"B" Is for Betsy.* (Harcourt, Brace & Company, 1939).

Heide, Florence Parry, illustrated by Edward Gorey. *The Shrinking of Treehorn.* (New York: Holiday House, 1971).

Hendry, Diana. *The Rainbow Watchers.* (New York: Knopf, 1989).

Hest, Amy. *Pajama Party.* (New York: Morrow Junior Books, 1992).

Hill, Eric. *Where's Spot?* (New York: Putnam, 1985).

Hoban, Tana. *Count and See.* (New York: Macmillan, 1972).

Hoban, Lillian. *Arthur's Honey Bear.* (New York: Harper & Row, 1972).

Hoff, Syd. *Barkley.* (New York: Harper & Row, 1975).

Hoff, Syd. *Chester.* (New York: Harper & Row, 1961).

Hoff, Syd. *Danny and the Dinosaur.* (Weston, CT: Weston Woods Studio, 1958, 1985).

Hopkins, Lee Bennett, illustrated by Megan Lloyd. *Surprises.* (New York: Harper & Row, 1984).

Houston, James. *Tikta'Liktak: An Eskimo Legend.* (New York: Harcourt, Brace & World, 1965).

Howe, James. *Pinky and Rex Go to Camp.* (New York/Toronto: Atheneum, Collier: Macmillan Canada, 1992).

Hurd, Edith Thacher. *Come and Have Fun.* (New York: Harper & Row, 1962).

Hurwitz, Johanna. *'E' Is for Elisa.* (New York: Morrow Junior Books, 1991).

Jonas, Ann. *Where Can It Be?* (New York: Greenwillow Books, 1986).

Kennedy, Richard, illustrated by Marcia Sewall. *Richard Kennedy: Collected Stories.* (New York: Harper & Row, 1987).

Khalsa. *I Want a Dog.* (New York: Clarkson N. Potter: Crown Publisher, 1987).

Kline, Suzy. *Horrible Harry in Room.* (New York: Viking Kestrel, 1988).

Krauss, Robert. *Whose Mouse Are You?* (New York: Macmillan, 1970).

Krementz, Jill. *A Very Young Dancer.* (New York: Knopf/Random House, 1976).

Kuskin, Karla. *Something Sleeping in the Hall.* (New York: Harper & Row, 1985).

Langstaff, John. *Oh, A-Hunting We Will Go.* (New York: Atheneum, 1974).

Lauber, Patricia. *Snakes Are Hunters.* (New York: T.Y. Crowell, 1988).

Le Gallienne, Eva, illustrated by Maurice Sendak. *Seven Tales By H.C Andersen: Translated from the Danish.* (New York: Harper & Row, 1959).

Le Sueur, Meridel, illustrated by Suzy Sansom. *Little Brother of the Wilderness: The Story of Johnny Appleseed.* (New York: Knopf, 1947).

Leverich, Kathleen, illustrated by Susan Condie Lamb. *Best Enemies Again.* (New York: Greenwillow Press, 1991).

Levinson, Riki, illustrated by Helen Cogancherry. *Dinnieabbiesister-r-r.* (Minneapolis, MN: Bradbury, 1987).

Levison, Nancy Smiler. *Clara and the Book Wagon.* (New York: Harper & Row, 1988).

Lindgren, Astrid, illustrated by Julie Brinkloe. *Lotta On Trouble Maker Street.* (New York: Macmillan, 1962).

Lindgren, Astrid. *Pippi Longstocking.* (New York: Viking Press, 1950).

Lindgren, Barbro. *Sam's Ball.* (New York: William Morrow, 1983).

Lindgren, Barbro. *Sam's Cookie.* (New York: William Morrow, 1982).

Lindgren, Barbro. *Sam's Wagon.* (New York: William Morrow, 1986).

Lobel, Arnold. *Mouse Tales.* (New York: Harper & Row, 1972).

Lobel, Arnold. *Owl at Home.* (New York: Harper & Row, 1975).

Lobel, Arnold. *Frog and Toad Together.* (New York: Harper & Row, 1972).

Lobel, Arnold. *Uncle Elephant.* (New York: Harper & Row, 1981).

Lopshire, Robert. *Put Me in the Zoo.* (Westminster, MD: Random House Educational Media, 1974).

Lovelace, Maud Hart, illustrated by Lois Lenski. *Betsy-Tacy.* (New York: Thomas Y. Crowell Company, 1940).

Lowrey, Janette (Sebring). *Six Silver Spoons.* (New York: Harper & Row, 1971).

Maris, Ron. *Are You There, Bear?* (New York: Greenwillow Books, 1984).

Mark, Jan. *Fun.* (New York: Viking Kestrel, 1987).

Marshall, James. *Rats on the Roof and Other Stories.* (New York: Dial Books for Young Readers, 1991).

Martin, Bill. *Brown Bear, Brown Bear, What Do You See?* (New York:

Holt, Rinehart, and Winston, 1983).

Martin, Bill. *Knots on a Counting Rope.* (New York: H. Holt, 1987).

Matthias, John. *I Love Cats.* (Chicago: Swallow Press, 1971).

Matthias, John. *Too Many Balloons.* (Chicago: Swallow Press, 1971).

McClintock, Mike. *What Have I Got?* (New York: Harper & Row, 1961).

McDaniel, Becky. *Katie Did It.* (Chicago: Childrens Press, 1993).

Miller, Margaret. *Whose Hat?* (New York: Greenwillow Books, 1988).

Miller, Margaret. *Whose Shoe?* (New York: Greenwillow Books, 1991).

Minarik, Else Holmelund, illustrated by Maurice Sendak. *Little Bear.* (New York: Harper, 1957).

Minarik, Else Holmelund. *Cat and Dog.* (New York: Harper, 1960).

Morris, Ann. *Bread Bread Bread.* (New York: Lothrop, Lee & Shepard Books, 1989).

Osborne, Mary P. *Dinosaurs Before Dark.* (New York: Random House, 1992).

Parish, Peggy, illustrated by Fritz Seibel. *Amelia Bedelia.* (New York: Harper & Row, 1963).

Parish, Peggy, illustrated by Marc Simont. *No More Monsters for Me.* (New York: Harper & Row, 1981).

Peek, Merle. *Mary Wore Her Red Dress.* (New York: Clarion Books, 1987).

Perkins, Al. *Hand, Hand, Fingers, Thumb.* (New York: Random House, 1969).

Petrie, Catherine. *Joshua James Likes Trucks.* (Chicago: Childrens Press, 1982).

Pinkwater, Daniel. *Roger's Umbrella.* (New York: Dutton, 1982).

Pinkwater, Daniel. *Guys From Space.* (New York: Macmillan, 1989).

Rappaport, Doreen. *The Boston Coffee Party.* (New York: Harper & Row, 1988).

Roffey, Maureen. *Home Sweet Home.* (Bantam, 1988).

Roop, Peter. *Buttons for General Washington.* (Minneapolis: Carolrhoda Books, 1986).

Roop, Connie and Peter, illustrated by Peter E. Hanson. *Keep the Lights Burning, Abbie.* (Minneapolis: Carolrhoda Books, 1985).

Ross, Pat. *M and M and The Mummy Mess.* (New York: Viking Kestrel, 1985).

Rounds, Glen. *Old Macdonald Had a Farm.* (New York: Holiday House, 1989).

Rylant, Cynthia. *Henry and Mudge in the Green Time.* (New York: Random House Video, 1988).

Rylant, Cynthia. *The Relatives Came.* (New York: Bradbury Press, 1985).

Sawicki, Norma Jean. *The Little Red House.* (New York: Lothrop, Lee & Shepard Books, 1989).

Schenk de Regniers, Beatrice., ed. *Sing a Song of Popcorn.* (New York: Scholastic, Inc., 1988).

Schwartz, Alvin. *All of Our Noses Are Here and Other Noodle Tales.* (New York: Harper & Row, 1982).

Schwartz, Alvin, illustrated by Dirk Zimmer. *In a Dark, Dark Room.* (New York: Harper & Row, 1984).

Shannon, George. *Stories to Solve: Folktales from Around the World.* (New York: Greenwillow Books, 1985).

Sharmat, Marjorie Weinman, illustrated by Marc Simont. *Nate the Great.* (New York: Coward, McCann & Geoghegan 1972).

Shaw, Charles. *It Looked Like Spilt Milk.* (New York: Harper, 1947).

Shaw, Nancy. *Sheep in a Shop.* (Boston: Houghton Mifflin, 1991).

Singer, Marily, illustrated by Jerry Pinkney. *Turtle in July.* (New York: Macmillan, 1989).

Slobodkina, Esphyr. *Caps for Sale.* (Sound Recording) (Weston, CT: Weston Woods Studios).

Stadler, John. *Snail Saves the Day.* (New York: Lothrop, Lee & Shepard Books, 1988).

Tafuri, Nancy. *Have You Seen My Duckling?* (New York: Greenwillow Books, 1984).

Tafuri, Nancy. *Spots, Feathers, and Curly Tails.* (New York: Greenwillow Books, 1988).

Tafuri, Nancy. *Who's Counting?* (New York: Greenwillow Books, 1986).

Testa, Fulvio. *If You Take a Paintbrush.* (New York: Dial Press, 1983).

Thaler, Mike, illustrated by Maxie Chambliss. *It's Me, Hippo!* (New York: Harper & Row, 1983).

Van de Wetering, Janwillem. *Hugh Pine.* (New York: Houghton Mifflin, 1980).

Watanabe, Shigeo. *I'm the King of the Castle.* (New York: Philomel Books, 1982).

Westcott, Nadine Bernard. *The Lady with the Alligator Purse.* (Boston: Joy Street Books, 1989).

Van Leeuwen, Jean, illustrated by Ann Schweninger. *Amanda Pig and Her Big Brother Oliver.* (New York: Dial Press, 1982).

Wheeler, Cindy. *Marmalade's Nap.* (New York: Knopf, 1983).

Wheeler, Cindy. *Snowy Day.* (New York: Knopf: Random House, 1982).

Wilder, Laura Ingalls, illustrated by Garth Williams. *Little House in the Big Woods.* (New York: Harper & Row, 1953).

Wildsmith, Brian. *The Cat on the Mat.* (New York: Franklin Watts, 1964).

Wildsmith, Brian. *Toot, Toot.* (New York: Franklin Watts, 1964).

Williams, Sue. *I Went Walking.* (San Diego: Harcourt Brace Jovanovich, 1990).

Willis, Val. *The Secret in the Match Box.* (New York: Farrar, Straus & Giroux, 1988).

Winter, Jeanette. *Follow the Drinking Gourd.* (New York: Knopf, 1988).

Wiseman, Bernard. *Morris and Boris: Three Stories.* (New York: Dodd, Mead, 1974).

Wittman, Sally. *Stepbrother Sabotage.* (New York: Coward-McCann, 1986).

Zemach, Margot. *The Three Wishes: An Old Story.* (New York: Farrar, Straus & Giroux, 1986).

INDEX